What Can You Do with a Major in

BUSINESS?

What Can You Do with a Major in

BUSINESS?

Real people.

Real jobs.

Real rewards.

Kate Shoup Welsh

Jennifer A. Horowitz,
Series Creator

WILEY

Wiley Publishing, Inc.

ISBN: 0-7645-7608-9

Library of Congress Cataloging-in-Publication data is available from the publisher upon request.

Printed in the United States of America

10 9 8 7 6 5 4 3 2 1

Book design by LeAndra Hosier
Cover design by Sandy St. Jacques
Book production by Wiley Publishing, Inc. Composition Services

WILEY

Table of Contents

Foreword

What can I do with a major in business?

Can you give me a list of jobs I can do if I major in business?

Should I major in X and minor in Y or major in Y and minor in X to be sure I'll get a great job?

How often I've heard these questions as a career counselor at a traditional liberal arts college. Concerns about "the major" are consuming to students from their first year through their last. At first it is the anxiety over choosing the "perfect" major; later it is concern that the major chosen may not have been the right decision.

Gone are the days when students felt they could major in anything they chose with no concern about their future careers. Managerial training programs that welcomed bright college graduates regardless of their academic backgrounds are rarely seen, and the world seems to get more and more specialized and require greater and greater focus and preparation from college graduates.

This series of books should ease much of the anxiety around the choice of major through its thoughtful exploration of possible career paths that lead directly from a specific major or which may at first glance seem completely unrelated. Much can be learned from the personal histories of individuals who majored in particular fields as well as from the rich resources in the Appendix.

Career development is a messy process. It can be seen as a dialogue between the self and the world. It involves interests, skills, values, and dreams. It requires an individual to be able to articulate her or his assets, whether they are transferable skills, abilities honed through jobs and internships, passions fueled by community service — and whatever one has chosen for a solid academic foundation — one's major.

— Jane Celwyn
Director of the Office of Career Development
Barnard College, New York

About This Book

This book is part of a series of major-based career guides. Here you will see how the book is organized and find out how to make it work for you. In the following sections, I describe the chapters you will find in this book. Feel free to read the chapters in whatever order is most helpful to you.

Chapter 1: Majoring in Business

This chapter outlines what students majoring in business can expect with regard to course work and requirements. You'll also find ways to tailor your education to help you land that dream job when you graduate—or at the very least, an entry-level position that puts you on the right path—by choosing a concentration during the course of your studies.

Chapter 2: Choosing a College

Knowing you want to study business can make choosing a college much easier. This chapter describes the most outstanding undergraduate business programs in the nation.

Chapter 3: Making the Most of Your Time at College

This chapter is designed to illustrate to business majors how to increase their chances of gainful employment upon graduation by maximizing their college experience.

Chapter 4: Attending Graduate School

Whether you received an undergraduate degree in business or in some other field, you may well decide that you want to pursue an MBA. This chapter is designed to help you decide whether an MBA is right for you, determine how obtaining an MBA can help you with your job search, discover what sort of undergraduate background and grades are required, find out how to obtain excellent letters of recommendation from professors and other sources, figure out how to pay for your schooling, and estimate how much time you can expect to devote to your studies. You'll also find information about the top MBA programs in the nation.

Chapter 5: Career Options for the Business Major

A business major acquires several skills and abilities that transfer well to any number of jobs in any number of industries. All these, plus the work ethic and self-discipline you're sure to develop during the course of your studies, will serve you well upon graduation. In this chapter, you'll get a glimpse of a few of your options.

Chapter 6: Breaking into the Job Market

This chapter is designed to help college students, recent grads, or anyone interested in changing careers find—and land—a great job in business.

Chapter 7: Case Studies

Meet six people who earned undergraduate degrees in business or who returned to school for an MBA. These people describe what they do and what they like and dislike about their jobs. They tell you how they got to where they are today and discuss their successes and mistakes so you can benefit from their experiences.

Appendix: Resources for the Business Major

Here you'll find a wealth of other information related to the business major, regardless of career, such as:

◆ Honor societies, with contact information

◆ Publications, with subscription information

◆ Websites that offer relevant information

You'll also find information on choosing the major and/or career that is right for you, such as:

◆ Self-administered aptitude tests and where to find them

◆ Books for further reading

After reading this book, I hope you will see that there are many ways to make a living with a major in business. Some may be the logical or even stereotypical careers associated with the major, while others are quite innovative, unusual, and perhaps ones you've never even heard of. But they all depend on the knowledge acquired from a major in business. Keep an open mind—you never know where life will take you!

## Chapter 1

Majoring in Business

Some students descend on college knowing just what they want to do with their lives. For them, choosing a major is easy! They simply determine which course of study will yield the credentials they need, and choose accordingly. If you're one of these lucky few—you know, for example, that you want to be an investment banker or CEO of a Fortune 500 company—and you've determined that a business major is your logical choice, then this chapter is for you. Here, you'll find out what types of courses you can expect to take as a general business major. You'll also discover ways to tailor your education to help you land that dream job when you graduate—or, at the very least, an entry-level position that puts you on the right path.

Getting the Major: A Typical Curriculum

Most students enter a business major program to both learn about business and to obtain a broad college education. To this end, you'll find that many undergraduate business programs are designed with a liberal arts curriculum in mind. The University of Pennsylvania's Wharton School is a perfect example. There, according to the school's website, students pursuing undergraduate business degrees have "the opportunity to focus on an integrated curriculum of business and liberal arts."

The same goes for the Haas School of Business at the University of California-Berkeley, where, according to the school's website, "course work is fully integrated with the university's liberal arts curriculum, allowing students to gain a broad perspective on business management and its environment."

The business-related course work, often referred to as the *business core,* typically includes foundational courses in the following disciplines:

- Accounting
- Computer applications
- Economics
- Finance
- Law
- Management
- Marketing
- Statistics

In addition to requiring business students to complete the business core, many schools require those pursuing a course of study in business to select a *concentration*—that is, a specific discipline in the field of business. Typical concentrations include, but are not limited to, the following:

- Accounting
- Economics
- Entrepreneurship
- Finance
- Health care administration
- International business
- Management
- Marketing
- Operations

◆ Statistics

◆ Technology

Of course, the available concentrations vary from school to school, and may include options not listed here. For example, some schools offer concentrations in biotechnology, real estate management, e-commerce, nonprofit management, and even livestock management.

To give you a sense of what types of course work you can expect to complete during your business studies, we have provided the curricula of two celebrated undergraduate business programs: The University of Pennsylvania's Wharton School (ranked number one in the nation by *U.S. News & World Report*) and Indiana University's Kelley School of Business (ranked number eleven in the nation by *U.S. News & World Report*). Of course, specific course work will vary from institution to institution, but this should at least give you a taste of what you can expect.

CURRICULUM FOR UNIVERSITY OF PENNSYLVANIA'S WHARTON SCHOOL

Students who complete their undergraduate studies at the University of Pennsylvania's Wharton School earn what's called a Wharton B.S. in Economics, which is the equivalent of a Bachelor's of Business Administration (BBA) or a Bachelor of Science in Business Administration (BSBA). Course work for the degree includes the following (some aspects of each course description are verbatim text that appears on the Wharton School's website):

General Education Requirement

Undergraduates at the Wharton School must complete at least 16 general education courses:

3 Foundation Courses

Students must take the following three business foundation courses:

◆ Economics 001 and 002: Microeconomics and Macroeconomics. Economics provides a basis for understanding what markets are and how they function.

◆ Calculus (Math 104). All students are required to take the first semester of Calculus. Math 104 assumes that students have had the equivalent of AB Calculus in high school and are familiar with concepts through applications of differentiation and basic integration techniques. Math, like economics, is an important tool in approaching business courses. Calculus will provide you with the background for other quantitative work in business courses.

7 Liberal Arts Courses

Students must take seven liberal arts courses in any of the following departments:

◆ Humanities

◆ Social Sciences

◆ Natural Sciences

1 Writing Course

All students must take a Writing About course to fulfill this requirement. These courses generally are numbered as English 001-009 and English 125. English 011, English for International Students, may also be used to fulfill the requirement if you are a student whose first language is not English. In addition, other departments, such as Philosophy and Women's Studies, offer Writing About courses, usually numbered 009. The *Fiction Writing Workshop,* the *Creative Writing Workshop,* and *Writing Across the University* do not satisfy the Wharton writing requirement, and AP credit in English cannot be used to fulfill this requirement.

5 Electives

These five elective courses can be anything you like—Bowling, Underwater Basket Weaving, or what have you. Smart business students, however, will choose electives that tie into their degree in some way. For example, if you hope to work in marketing, consider taking electives that enhance your understanding of the culture in which you plan to work.

Foreign Language Requirement

Unlike at many business schools, students at the Wharton school are not exempt from fulfilling a foreign language requirement—which makes sense, given the global nature of business today. Penn offers instruction in more than 100 languages; pick one that relates to your business degree in some way. For example, if you hope to work for a company with ties in Japan, then some understanding of the Japanese language will boost your résumé tremendously.

Business Education Requirement

In addition to fulfilling the abovementioned general education and foreign language requirements, students at Wharton must complete the following business courses:

1 Management 100 Course

Leadership and Communication in Groups (Management 100) is required. Because the development of leadership and communication skills is one of the central objectives of the Wharton undergraduate curriculum, this required course provides a very important forum for understanding your current abilities in these areas and how to improve them.

9 Business Fundamental Courses

The nine required business fundamental courses are as follows:

◆ Accounting 101 and 102: Principles of Accounting. Usually taken in the sophomore year, these introductory courses in financial and managerial accounting provide a broad-based understanding of how an organization reports on its financial position and the decisions leaders must make when creating financial reports. Accounting has been described as the "language of business." A thorough knowledge of its principles is necessary for all business professionals.

◆ Statistics 101 and 102: Introductory Business Statistics. Two semesters of Statistics are required, following completion of the Calculus requirement. These courses are focused on statistical methods used in many upper-level courses, especially Finance.

◆ Corporate Finance (Finance 100) and Monetary Economics and the Global Economy (Finance 101): Finance 100 provides an introduction to the theory and methods that are relevant for financial decisions made by firms. Finance 101 is an intermediate-level course about macroeconomics and the global economy in which firms operate.

◆ Management 101: Introduction to Management. This course addresses contemporary management challenges stemming from changing organizational structures, complex environmental conditions, new technological developments, and increasingly diverse workforces. It highlights critical management issues involving planning, organizing, controlling, and leading an organization. This course will help students understand some of the issues involved in managing and being managed and equip students to become effective contributors to organizations.

◆ Marketing 101: Introduction to Marketing. Every organization is faced with the challenge of how to communicate with the world at large about its mission, products, and services. An introduction to the methods of marketing teaches students how to think systematically about this challenge and how organizations can address their needs in this area.

◆ Operations and Information Management 101: Introduction to the Computer as an Analysis Tool. This course will introduce you to Microsoft Excel and other technology that will be very useful for both academic and professional purposes.

4 Business Depth Courses
Students must complete four upper-level courses in one of eighteen concentrations (Accounting, Actuarial Science, Business and Public Policy, Entrepreneurship, Environmental Policy and Management, Finance, Global Analysis, Health Care Management and Policy, Insurance and Risk Management, Legal Studies, Management, Managing Electronic Commerce, Marketing, Marketing and Communication, Operations and Information Management, Real Estate, Statistics, and Individualized).

3 Business Breadth Courses
Students must complete three upper-level courses in disciplines outside their concentration.

Environment of Business Requirement
Finally, students must complete these course requirements in order to earn a degree in business from the Wharton School:

3 Societal Context Courses

Students must complete the following three context courses:

◆ Legal Studies 101: Introduction to Law and Legal Process. This course provides an overall introduction to the American legal system. Any leader of an organization that does business in the United States must understand this legal environment to conduct business successfully.

◆ Legal Studies 210: Corporate Responsibility and Ethics. Every member of a business organization is faced with making ethical decisions. This course provides a structure for thinking through problems and developing appropriate responses when ethical challenges arise.

◆ Business and Public Policy 203: Business and the Global Political Environment. Organizations around the world must deal not only with their clients, customers, and shareholders, but also with the communities in which they are located and with the governments of the entities in which they are housed. This course discusses how firms respond to various regulatory and political forces in the external environment.

1 Organizational Context Course

Students must choose one of the following two organizational context courses for completion:

◆ Management 104: Industrial Relations and Human Resource Management. One of the most important managerial tasks is developing rewarding and productive relationships with co-workers and employees. This course teaches students how to approach issues in the management of human resources at all levels of an organization.

◆ Insurance 205: Risk Management. All firms must cope with risks: financial risks, risks associated with destruction of property, and risks associated with variability in human behavior. This course discusses the risks companies face and how they can best plan to minimize the negative effects of various kinds of risks.

3 Global Context Courses
Students must complete three courses that focus on international content.

CURRICULUM FOR INDIANA UNIVERSITY'S KELLEY SCHOOL OF BUSINESS

Students who complete their undergraduate studies at Indiana University's Kelley School of Business earn a BBA. Course work for the degree includes the following (some aspects of each course description are verbatim text that appears on the Kelley School of Business website):

General Education Requirement

Kelley School of Business majors must complete at least 62 credit hours outside of business and economics course work. This includes the following courses.

Communications (8 or 9 Credit Hours)

◆ ENG-W 131 Elementary Composition or an approved English composition option (2–3 credits)

◆ CMCL-C 121 Public Speaking (3 credits)

◆ BUS-X 204 Business Communications (3 credits)

Mathematics (6 or 7 Credit Hours)

◆ MATH-M 118 Finite Mathematics (3 credits)

◆ MATH-M 119 Brief Survey of Calculus I (3 credits) or MATH-M 211 Calculus I (4 credits)

International Dimension (6 Credit Hours)
The international dimension requirement may be fulfilled in any one of the following four ways:

◆ Language: A minimum of 6 credit hours of a language at the 200 level or above.

◆ International Business and Economics: A minimum of 6 credit hours from the following list:

- ◆ BUS-D 301 The International Business Environment (3 credits)
- ◆ BUS-D 302 International Business: Operations of International Enterprises (3 credits)
- ◆ BUS-L 411 International Business Law (3 credits)
- ◆ BUS-F 494 International Finance (3 credits)
- ◆ BUS-G 494 Public Policy and the International Economy (3 credits)
- ◆ BUS-M 401 International Marketing (3 credits)
- ◆ BUS-X 330 International Communication Strategies (3 credits)
- ◆ ECON-E 303 Survey of International Economics (3 credits)
- ◆ ECON-E 331 International Trade (3 credits)
- ◆ ECON-E 332 International Monetary Economics (3 credits)
- ◆ ECON-E 337 Economic Development (3 credits)
- ◆ ECON-E 386 Soviet-Type Economies in Transition (3 credits)

◆ Approved Overseas Programs: Participation in any approved overseas program of Indiana University (minimum 6 credits) will fulfill this requirement.

◆ Area Studies: Selection of two approved courses (minimum 6 credits) from one of the following area studies programs:

- ◆ African Studies
- ◆ Central Eurasian Studies
- ◆ East Asian Studies
- ◆ Latin American and Caribbean Studies
- ◆ Near Eastern Studies
- ◆ Russian and East European Studies
- ◆ West European Studies

Note: International students studying at the Kelley School of Business should see a business advisor to obtain a waiver for the International Dimension Requirement.

Core (27 Credit Hours)
Students may choose one of two alternatives to complete the 27 credit-hour core:

◆ The Distribution Option: Complete 15 credit hours of course work offered by the College of Arts and Sciences in Arts and Humanities, Social and Historical Studies, or Natural and Mathematical Sciences, with a minimum of 6 credit hours at the 300/400 level (with the exception of Natural and Mathematical Sciences, which requires 6 credit hours at the 200 level or higher). In addition, complete 6 credit hours in each of the other two College of Arts and Sciences areas not selected for the 15 credit-hour requirement.

◆ The Field Specialization Option: Students may complete one of the field specializations listed below by completing 27 credit hours taking any courses from the departments or schools within the chosen field. At least 6 of the 27 required credit hours must be at the 300/400 level for all but the science and technology field, which requires at least 6 credit hours at the 200 level or above.

   ◆ African Studies

   ◆ American Sign Language

   ◆ Arts and Social Services

   ◆ Astronomy

   ◆ Biology

   ◆ Central Eurasian Studies

   ◆ Chemistry

   ◆ Classical Studies

   ◆ Communication

   ◆ Communication and Culture

- Computer Science
- East Asian Studies
- English
- Environmental Studies
- Fine Arts
- French/Italian Studies
- Geological Sciences
- Germanic Studies
- Global Studies and Languages
- History and Philosophy of Science
- India Studies
- Jewish Studies
- Journalism
- Latin American and Caribbean Studies
- Mathematics
- Medical Science
- Music
- Near Eastern Studies
- Philosophy
- Physics
- Public and Environmental Affairs
- Religious Studies
- Russian and East European Studies
- Science and Technology
- Social Work
- Spanish/Portuguese Studies

- ◆ Speech and Hearing Sciences
- ◆ Telecommunications
- ◆ Theatre
- ◆ West European Studies

Supplemental Hours
Students may choose courses from throughout the university, excluding Kelley School of Business and Department of Economics courses, to complete the 62 credit-hour general-education component. The number of credit hours each student will take for this will depend on how other categories of the general-education component are met.

Business Component
Fundamentals

- ◆ BUS-A 100 Business Accounting Skills (1 credit)
- ◆ BUS-A 201 Introduction to Financial Accounting (3 credits)
- ◆ BUS-A 202 Introduction to Managerial Accounting (3 credits)
- ◆ BUS-K 201 The Computer in Business (3 credits)
- ◆ BUS-L 201 Legal Environment of Business (3 credits)
- ◆ BUS-X 201 Technology (3 credits)
- ◆ BUS-X 220 Career Perspectives (2 credits)
- ◆ BUS-G 202 Business and Economic Strategy in the Public Arena (3 credits)
- ◆ ECON-E 201 Introduction to Microeconomics (3 credits)
- ◆ ECON-E 370 Statistical Analysis in Economics and Business (3 credits)

Junior Year

- ◆ BUS-Z 302 Managing and Behavior in Organizations (3 credits)
- ◆ ECON-E 202 Introduction to Macroeconomics (3 credits)

Senior Year

◆ BUS-X 420 Business Career Planning and Placement (2 credits)

Integrative Core (12 Credits)

◆ BUS-F 370 Financial Management (3 credits)

◆ BUS-J 370 Strategic Management (3 credits)

◆ BUS-M 370 Marketing Management (3 credits)

◆ BUS-P 370 Operations Management (3 credits)

Business Concentrations

In addition to fulfilling the general-education component and the business component requirements previously listed, students in the Kelley School of Business select one or more of the following concentrations:

◆ Accounting

◆ Business Economics and Public Policy

    ◆ Economic Consulting Track

    ◆ Public Policy Analysis Track

◆ Business Information Systems

◆ Business Law

◆ Business Process Management

◆ Computer Information Systems

◆ Entrepreneurship

◆ Finance

◆ Finance-Real Estate

◆ International Business

◆ Management

◆ Marketing

◆ Production/Operations Management

Skills Required to Succeed with This Major

If you're a good communicator, like to lead, are well organized, prefer working in a team environment, enjoy working with numbers, and know your way around a computer, then you're well on your way to enjoying success in your business studies. In addition, a general awareness of current events will serve you well. Often, news at the local, national, and international levels can shed a bright light on business trends. As an obvious example, the use of airliners by terrorists on September 11, 2001, foreshadowed a steep decline in the airline business. Other less-obvious examples of the connection between business and world events can be found nearly every day.

Challenges Associated with Choosing This Major

Every major has its pros and cons. For English majors, one pitfall is the volume of written work one is required to complete. For engineering majors, the most serious challenge involves the sheer complexity of the subject matter at hand. Fortunately for you, the business major, neither of these precise challenges applies. Written papers are the exception, not the rule. And although business studies are by no means a walk in the park, they tend to be more grounded in the world of simple common sense than, say, studies in topics such as quantum physics, mechanical engineering, or organic chemistry.

Instead, chief among the challenges associated with pursuing a course of study in business is its emphasis on the lecture format—which, depending on the speaking abilities of the lecturer, can make it difficult to sustain one's enthusiasm for the topic at hand. Fortunately, rather than being required to simply listen and take notes, students are asked to analyze actual business problems presented in case studies, develop solutions, and defend their conclusions—much as one must do in a real-life business environment.

However, students who lack any one of the skills listed in the preceding section—namely, communication, leadership, organizational, people, computer, or mathematical skills—may find their business studies particularly challenging.

How the World Views This Major

In "Fresh Writing," a journal of outstanding essays written by students of the first-year writing course at Notre Dame, it's observed that "Especially at the University of Notre Dame, certain majors are believed to be more credible than others. For example, those found in the fields of mathematics and science are perceived to be highly difficult and time consuming, and therefore command a great deal of respect in the college arena." The essay continues, "On the other hand, majors found in Arts and Letters and Business are deemed to be quite a bit easier, less stressful, and as a result are often scorned." Indeed, one student interviewed by the essay's author asserted that the business major "is for slackers who just want to get by."

Employers, however, have a slightly different view of business majors—especially those who have made the most of their studies, as we'll discuss in Chapter 3. In general, the average employer views business majors as very solid job candidates, thanks to their broad-based education and business know-how.

Current Prospective for Future of Recent Graduates

Students equipped with a business degree entering the job market in 2005 can expect to find mixed results due to the economic difficulties that have plagued the United States since the collapse of the dot-com boom and the terrorist attacks on September 11, 2001. Although the general consensus on Wall Street has been that the national economy is in the midst of "an early growing period," the UCLA Anderson Forecast, recognized as one of the most accurate and unbiased forecasting organizations in the nation, warned in September 2004 of a possible recession in 2005 or 2006.

Likewise, University of Maryland economist Peter Morici, former chief economist for the U.S. International Trade Commission, noted in

October 2004 that "Poor economic policies are keeping Americans from finding better jobs and enjoying the rising living standards promised by new technology." Given this, Morici predicts that throughout 2005, the U.S. economy will continue to perform below its potential, growing at an annual rate of about 3.5 percent.

Now the good news: Students with business majors may find themselves with an edge over other college graduates when competing for those jobs that *are* available. Why? Because business majors already have some understanding of how business works, and as a result may require less training in entry-level positions than their graduating counterparts. Indeed, one study conducted in Minnesota revealed that 66 percent of employers surveyed declared that they were interested in hiring business majors during 2004 and 2005. (For information about which types of industries tend to hire business majors, see Chapter 5.)

Choosing a College

Choosing a college is among the most important—not to mention daunting—decisions you'll make during your life. After all, your choice of college, and how well you do there, can affect your career prospects for the duration of your working life! It's no wonder, then, that so many college prospects become overwhelmed by the process of deciding which school to attend; their very future hangs in the balance.

You, however, are among the lucky ones. Why? Because unlike many college-bound men and women, you already know what you want to study: business. Obviously, then, you'll want to focus your efforts on applying to schools that offer outstanding business programs for undergraduate students. That's where this chapter comes in. Here, you'll uncover the top undergraduate business programs in the nation, and learn a bit about several of the top schools.

The Cream of the Crop: Pinpointing the Best Undergraduate Programs

Just which schools offer the best business programs for undergraduate students? Some may surprise you. In the list that follows, you'll find an intriguing blend of private colleges and state-funded universities, of large public schools and small private ones, of schools in nearly every pocket of the continental United States. For all their differences, however, these schools have one thing in common: an uncommonly strong undergraduate business program.

The following list was compiled from two primary sources: *U.S. News & World Report*'s "Best Undergraduate Business Programs," a subsection of that magazine's "America's Best Colleges 2005"; and *Business Week*'s list of the top-30 MBA programs in the United States. (Note: Although the *Business Week* list contains MBA programs only, we found it instructive nonetheless.)

Without further ado, here's our list of the top-10 undergraduate business schools in the nation (note that number 3 is a tie):

1. University of Pennsylvania's Wharton School

2. MIT's Sloan School of Management

3. University of California-Berkeley's Haas School of Business

3. University of Michigan-Ann Arbor's Ross School of Business

4. New York University's Stern School of Business

5. Carnegie Mellon University's Tepper School of Business

6. University of North Carolina-Chapel Hill's Kenan-Flagler School of Business

7. University of Texas-Austin's McCombs School of Business

8. University of Southern California's Marshall School of Business

9. University of Virginia's McIntire School of Commerce

For more information about each of these schools, read on!

UNIVERSITY OF PENNSYLVANIA'S WHARTON SCHOOL
http://undergrad.wharton.upenn.edu

The University of Pennsylvania, located in Philadelphia, touts the top-ranked undergraduate business program in the nation through its world-renowned Wharton School, founded in 1881. At the Wharton School, students experience an integrated curriculum of business and liberal arts that is designed to provide students with an international perspective. Graduates of the Wharton School at Penn have enjoyed careers as CEOs, ambassadors, writers, physicians, and lawyers, finding

| University of Pennsylvania Specs (2004–05) ||||
# of Undergraduate Students	Total Annual Costs	Scholarships	Loans
9,724	$42,100	Yes	Yes

work at such firms as Goldman Sachs, the University of Pennsylvania, Citigroup/Salomon Smith Barney, Merrill Lynch, and more. The university's career-counseling services expedite the job-search process for graduates by offering co-op education, on-campus job interviews, internships, résumé assistance, career/job search classes, an alumni network, interest-inventory, and interview training.

MASSACHUSETTS INSTITUTE OF TECHNOLOGY'S SLOAN SCHOOL OF MANAGEMENT

http://mitsloan.mit.edu/undergrad

Situated across the Charles River from Boston, MIT, located in the heart of scenic Cambridge, is both noted for its intense learning environment and its playful nature. Witness: In addition to noting the number of Nobel Laureates in the MIT community (57), the Institute's website cites how many red-tailed hawks call the campus home ("at least 4").

MIT's undergraduate Management Science program, a component of the Institute's Sloan School of Management, employs tools and techniques from such diverse fields as mathematics, engineering, information technology, and psychology to imbue in students the skills they'll need to become the business leaders of the future. Graduates from the program enjoy success in a broad range of fields, from Web-based commerce to financial engineering.

| MIT Specs (2004–05) ||||
# of Undergraduate Students	Total Annual Costs	Scholarships	Loans
4,112	$42,700	Yes	Yes

UNIVERSITY OF CALIFORNIA-BERKELEY'S HAAS SCHOOL OF BUSINESS

www.haas.berkeley.edu/undergrad

The Haas School of Business at the University of California-Berkeley has offered a superb business education for more than 100 years. Known for its diverse and talented faculty and staff, students, and alumni, the Haas School of Business focuses on cooperative teamwork, with course work that is fully integrated with the university's liberal arts curriculum.

That the Haas School of Business offers one of the top-ranked undergraduate business programs in the nation is but one reason to consider attending the University of California-Berkeley. Other reasons include the town's cultural diversity, beautiful parks, stunning landscape, temperate climate, great restaurants and shopping, and proximity to San Francisco, Oakland, and the Silicon Valley.

University of California-Berkeley Specs (2004–05)			
# of Undergraduate Students	*Total Annual Costs*	*Scholarships*	*Loans*
23,206	$21,260 (resident) $38,260 (nonresident)	Yes	Yes

UNIVERSITY OF MICHIGAN-ANN ARBOR'S ROSS SCHOOL OF BUSINESS

www.bus.umich.edu/Academics/BBAprogram

In addition to upholding a reputation as one of the world's finest public research universities, the University of Michigan is known for its picturesque campus and diverse cultural offerings. Indeed, in any given week, students can enjoy watching first-rate athletic events, exploring fascinating museum exhibitions, and listening to lectures by world-renowned speakers in varied fields of expertise.

University of Michigan Specs (2004–05)			
# of Undergraduate Students	Total Annual Costs	Scholarships	Loans
24,517	$17,072 (resident) $35,058 (nonresident)	Yes	Yes

Within that grand scheme is the University's Ross School of Business, a close-knit community featuring top-notch professors and facilities. In addition to receiving cutting-edge instruction in every area of business, students in the Ross School of Business's undergraduate program can enjoy interdisciplinary learning in a wide range of fields.

NEW YORK UNIVERSITY'S STERN SCHOOL OF BUSINESS
http://w4.stern.nyu.edu/ug

One could argue that there is no better place in the nation to study business than in New York City. Indeed, the city is home to the New York and American Stock Exchanges; in addition, as noted on the Stern School of Business's website, "virtually all major industries and corporations have either their headquarters or a major facility in the metropolitan area, offering you unprecedented opportunities for internships and part-time employment with leading New York businesses, as well as professional offerings upon graduation." Due to its proximity to the headquarters of such global firms as American Express, General Electric, J.P. Morgan, and the like, NYU has the unique ability to host on-campus seminars, conferences, and luncheons that enable students to connect and network with top-level executives, all while pursuing a course of study that thoroughly prepares them to engage in the business of tomorrow.

NYU Specs (2004–05)			
# of Undergraduate Students	Total Annual Costs	Scholarships	Loans
19,506	$43,185	Yes	Yes

Carnegie Mellon Specs (2004–05)			
# of Undergraduate Students	**Total Annual Costs**	**Scholarships**	**Loans**
5,484	$41,780	Yes	Yes

CARNEGIE MELLON UNIVERSITY'S TEPPER SCHOOL OF BUSINESS

http://web.gsia.cmu.edu/default.aspx?id=140993

Carnegie Mellon's co-founder, Scottish-born Andrew Carnegie, is known primarily for two things: enjoying tremendous success in business in the steel industry, and, later, philanthropically disbursing his substantial fortune to construct libraries in small towns nationwide in the hopes of enabling others to better their fortunes through learning. It's no wonder, then, that Carnegie Mellon is known both for its research strengths and for its outstanding business school, the Tepper School of Business. At Carnegie Mellon's Tepper School, located in beautiful Pittsburgh, students benefit from an impressive student-to-professor ratio, a diverse student body, and an innovative curriculum. Course work emphasizes analytical decision-making and creative problem-solving with a global focus.

UNIVERSITY OF NORTH CAROLINA-CHAPEL HILL'S KENAN-FLAGLER BUSINESS SCHOOL

www.kenan-flagler.unc.edu/Programs/BSBA

The nation's oldest public university, the University of North Carolina-Chapel Hill has long enjoyed an excellent academic reputation—and

University of North Carolina-Chapel Hill Specs (2004–05)			
# of Undergraduate Students	**Total Annual Costs**	**Scholarships**	**Loans**
16,144	$12,050 (resident) $25,148 (nonresident)	Yes	Yes

its Kenan-Flagler Business School is no exception. Founded in 1919 as the School of Commerce, the Kenan-Flagler School's undergraduate curriculum involves a broad-based liberal-arts business education to prepare students for the global nature of today's business climate. Learning is not limited to the classroom, however; the annual Undergraduate Business Symposium provides students with an exciting opportunity to exchange ideas with executives and faculty alike.

UNIVERSITY OF TEXAS-AUSTIN'S McCOMBS SCHOOL OF BUSINESS

www.mccombs.utexas.edu/udean

The University of Texas-Austin's McCombs School of Business has strong programs in every discipline of business, with its innovative technology, management, and accounting curricula deserving special praise. In addition, the school enables students to select market-driven specializations in such fields as energy finance, customer insight, and private equity. Graduates with BBAs from the McCombs School of Business have found great success in the areas of finance, consulting, and marketing.

Located in downtown Austin, the capital of Texas, the 350-acre University of Texas-Austin campus offers easy access not only to a top-ranked business education, but also to museums, outdoor life, entertainment venues, and more.

University of Texas-Austin Specs (2004–05)			
# of Undergraduate Students	Total Annual Costs	Scholarships	Loans
38,383	$17,488 (resident) $25,192 (nonresident)	Yes	Yes

UNIVERSITY OF SOUTHERN CALIFORNIA'S MARSHALL SCHOOL OF BUSINESS

www.marshall.usc.edu/web/Undergraduate.cfm?doc_id=3419

For more than 80 years, the Marshall School of Business at the University of Southern California, located in the heart of Los Angeles, has taught

University of Southern California Specs (2004–05)			
# of Undergraduate Students	Total Annual Costs	Scholarships	Loans
16,381	$41,774	Yes	Yes

students to think analytically and creatively, to develop management and leadership skills, and to learn how companies function. The school's global focus is enhanced by its diverse student body, featuring scholars from more than 100 countries. Upon completing their studies, Marshall graduates enjoy networking with some 67,000 alumni in 44 nations worldwide.

UNIVERSITY OF VIRGINIA'S MCINTIRE SCHOOL OF COMMERCE

www.commerce.virginia.edu/academic_programs/ undergraduate/undergraduate-genl.html

In their book *Cities Ranked and Rated*, authors Bert Sperling and Peter Sander cite Charlottesville, Virginia—the home of the University of Virginia—as the best place to live in the United States. Overlooking the Rivanna River, the picturesque city boasts a wide array of cultural activities and close proximity to a spectacular national park. For its part, the University of Virginia has earned its share of awards. Since 1993, the university has been named the nation's best public university by *U.S. News & World Report* magazine some six times. Yet another honor demonstrates the campus's unique loveliness: In 1987, the University of Virginia grounds was named a World Heritage site by UNESCO; other locations to receive the honor include the Taj Mahal, Versailles, and the Great Wall of China.

The university's founder, Thomas Jefferson, believed strongly in the importance of a liberal arts education. This stance is reflected in the curriculum of the University of Virginia's McIntire School of Commerce, where students spend the first two years of their academic career completing both liberal arts course work and business prerequisites. In their fourth year, however, students narrow their business studies to one or more concentrations: accounting, finance, information technology, international business, management, or marketing.

# of Undergraduate Students	Total Annual Costs	Scholarships	Loans
	University of Virginia Specs (2004–05)		
13,829	$15,160 (resident) $31,260 (nonresident)	Yes	Yes

Evaluating Other Schools

If, for whatever reason, the schools listed here don't meet your needs—perhaps you are obligated to stay close to home, or your finances won't permit the tuition assessed by these institutions—don't fret. Just because a school isn't in the top 10 or even the top 20 doesn't mean you can't leverage your education there to achieve your goals. In addition, certain business programs may excel at a particular discipline—say, accounting—but not be terribly distinguished overall. If accounting is your area of interest, one such program may well be the place for you. The bottom line? Don't be discouraged if your circumstances prevent you from attending one of the schools listed here. When you're armed with a business degree from *any* accredited, reputable institution, the sky is the limit.

Apply Yourself: Tips for Completing Your College Applications

Under the best of circumstances, applying for college is an arduous process. You must gather recommendations from teachers, employers, or other adults who believe in you. You must obtain your high-school transcript. You must ensure that your test scores—the SAT I, the SAT II, or the ACT, plus any AP tests you take—are forwarded to the colleges of your choice. If you need financial aid, you must submit forms as needed. And of course, you must complete any essays and application forms required by the institution to which you wish to apply—a task made even more difficult if you intend to apply to multiple schools. It's enough to intimidate even the most organized of students.

To help you through the trials of applying to college, consider the following tips:

◆ Be aware of deadlines! You may be applying to schools with different application-submission deadlines. Make sure you know when each application is due and complete it accordingly. Likewise, make sure you submit your financial-aid applications on time.

◆ When requesting recommendations and other materials, such as test scores and transcripts, make sure you give those helping you adequate time to complete their tasks. In other words, don't corner your guidance counselor on the Friday before your application is due to request a transcript. Plan ahead!

◆ If you are applying to multiple schools, see if any of them use what's known as the *Common Application*. If so, you can complete one copy of the Common Application, photocopy it, and send it to any participating colleges, which can save you time. Be aware, though, that some schools that accept the Common Application do expect you to submit supplemental application materials; check with each school's admissions office for specific requirements.

◆ If the multiple schools to which you are applying do not accept the Common Application, consider creating a "personal profile" as a sort of cheat sheet for filling out your applications. This cheat sheet might include information about any awards you've received, activities you've engaged in, and other personal information, such as your passions or hobbies. Not only does the sheet serve as reference material as you fill out each college application, but it can also help you pinpoint the perfect topic for your college essay.

◆ Do not submit documents or other materials that are not requested by your prospective school's admissions office.

◆ Always type your college applications rather than filling them out longhand. If a school to which you apply enables you to submit an online application, do so. This is especially useful if the application-submission deadline is imminent; applying online eliminates the lag time that occurs when items are sent via mail.

◆ Most colleges require you to pay an application fee. If you can demonstrate financial need, however, you may be able to have the fee waived. Contact your prospective school's admissions office for more information.

◆ Be sure to proofread your applications and essay carefully. Then, even if you're certain everything is correct, ask someone else, such as a teacher, counselor, parent, or friend, to proofread your application and essay as well.

◆ Choose an essay topic that illustrates what's important to you and why, and write clearly and succinctly.

Tips for Transfer Students

If you are currently enrolled in an academic institution that does not satisfy your interest in business, or if you have attended college but did not complete your degree, you may decide to transfer to a different college or university to pursue your studies. Whether you are currently enrolled at a four-year Ivy League institution, a large state university, a private liberal arts college, or even a local community college, if you wish to apply to a college or university as a transfer student, a few special considerations may apply:

◆ In general, students who have received failing, conditional, or incomplete grades at their current institution will not be admitted as transfer students at new institutions. Likewise, if you have been barred from attending school for disciplinary reasons, chances are you won't be eligible for admittance as a transfer student to another school.

◆ The number of credits you've completed often affects what types of items you must submit when applying to a new school as a transfer student. For example, if you've completed 30 or fewer hours of course work, you may be asked to supply additional documentation to help admissions officers determine whether to accept your application.

◆ Some schools, such as MIT, don't permit you to transfer if you've spent less than one year at another post-high school academic institution. Other schools, like Penn, permit you to transfer after only one semester, but not at mid-year; that is, you must start as a first-semester freshman the subsequent September. Still other schools refuse admissions to prospective transfer students who have completed fewer than 60 transferable credits—that is, students who have not completed their sophomore-level studies are not granted admission.

◆ Prospective transfer students who are within three semesters of acquiring a bachelor's degree elsewhere will be denied admission at some schools. Other schools, such as the University of Texas-Austin, do admit such students, but require them to complete an additional 60 hours of course work—two full years—before graduating, regardless of how many credits they accumulated elsewhere.

◆ In many schools, the transfer application process is more competitive than regular admissions. That means if you decide to transfer, you must work hard beforehand to ensure that your grades at your current institution are as high as possible. Other schools have more flexible admissions policies for transfer students; at Cal-Berkeley, for example, transfer students comprised nearly one-third of the Fall 2004 class.

◆ Some schools, such as the University of North Carolina at Chapel Hill, require transfer students who are interested in majoring in business to complete at least one semester in the College of Arts and Sciences before applying for admission to that degree program. Other schools, such as Penn's Wharton School and NYU's Stern School of Business, prohibit transfer students from doing so; that is, prospective transfer students *must* apply as business majors. They may not gain admission as, say, English majors and then change their major to business after admittance.

◆ Many schools require prospective transfer students to declare a major upon applying; applications are evaluated accordingly. Other schools require prospective transfer students to declare their major upon application only if they intend to transfer as a junior.

◆ Because many schools require prospective transfer students to declare their major upon application, admission deadlines and requirements may vary by major. Be certain you understand the requirements for *your* major.

◆ Because many sophomore-level students haven't yet committed to a major, there tend to be extra slots available for incoming sophomore-level transfer students in certain major programs. By the time prospective transfer students reach their junior year, however, those extra slots are often filled by students who are already enrolled. For this reason, students interested in transferring after their freshman year may enjoy greater odds of admission than students who are farther along in their studies. This is especially so for schools requiring prospective transfer students to declare a major upon application.

◆ Because transferring credits can be problematic, your overall college experience may be prolonged if you transfer. For example, MIT notes on its website that "transfer students typically lose at least one semester of course work."

Back to School: Special Considerations for Adult Learners

If you are 24 years of age or older; are a veteran of the armed services; are returning to school after four or more years of employment, home-making, or another activity; or assume multiple roles in addition to that of student, such as parent, spouse, employee, or what have you, then you are an *adult learner.* Adult learners, sometimes referred to as *nontraditional students,* typically return to school with a particular goal in mind, which often makes them more focused and dedicated than their younger, more traditional student counterparts. Life circumstances for such students, however, often make attending school difficult. For example, financial or family considerations may create obstacles to learning. If you are one such student, you'll want to take particular care in choosing the undergraduate business program that's right for you. In particular, you should consider the following:

◆ Does the school offer day-care services?

◆ Does the school provide housing for older students? Does it accommodate families?

◆ Does the school grant credits for life or work experience?

◆ Does the school offer support services or groups to help you connect with other students like you?

◆ Does the school offer counseling services for adult learners to help them transition into student life?

◆ Does the school offer a special orientation series geared toward adult learners?

◆ Does the school offer financial aid for nontraditional students?

◆ Does the school allow for flexible scheduling to better enable you to fulfill your work, home, and school responsibilities?

## Chapter 3

Making the Most of Your Time at College

Recently, an employment website called iseek.com (the product of a partnership involving, among other organizations, the University of Minnesota and the Minnesota Department of Employment and Economic Development) asked employers what qualifications recent college graduates should possess in order to be considered for employment. Here's how employers responded:

◆ Internship experience/previous relevant work experience

◆ Participation in campus organizations

◆ A GPA of 3.0 or higher

◆ Volunteer experience

Put another way, it could be said that the employers surveyed were really looking for candidates who had made the most of their time at college. This chapter is designed to illustrate to the business major how to increase his or her chances of gainful employment upon graduation by maximizing the college experience.

Finding Internships

An internship offers low-level (typically), full-time work experience that helps college students, recent college graduates, and anyone seeking to change careers gain experience—and make contacts—in their chosen field. Internships are typically not-for-pay endeavors, although some paid internships do exist. Note you may be able to receive academic credit for any internships you complete. Most internships take place during the summer, although you may be able to find a position during the fall or spring semester.

With more and more students completing internships, these positions are practically becoming a prerequisite for anyone looking for a top job after college. Indeed, as noted in the Career Planning area on About.com, "employers are coming to expect to see [an internship] listed on the résumés of potential employees." If your goal is to parlay your business degree into the job of your dreams, then you'll want to seriously consider completing at least one internship during your college years. (In fact, your school may require it of you.) And if you impress your bosses during your internship, you may just find yourself hired on full time when you graduate.

Just how does one find an internship? Whatever your major, the following resources can prove helpful:

◆ *Your college's career center.* Regardless of what type of internship you seek, your career center should be your first stop. Savvy counselors can give you the scoop on what's out there and how to successfully apply.

◆ *www.princetonreview.com/cte/search/careerSearch.asp.* Using the Princeton Review's Online Internship Database is a great way to find an internship. You can search for internships by location, field of interest, eligibility requirements, and more.

◆ *www.monstertrak.com.* This site, a division of the ubiquitous job-search site Monster.com, connects students and alumni with employers who offer internships. (Note that your college must be a MonsterTRAK partner in order for you to use the resources on this site.)

- *www.internweb.com.* If you're no longer in school or if your college's career center isn't up to snuff, try visiting this free site. It acts as a connection point for students and employers and provides a searchable listing of available internships.

- *www.internjobs.com.* This subsidiary of Jobs.com is a global database of internships for students, recent college grads, and career changers.

- *www.bigapplehead.com.* If you're interested in completing an internship in New York, Washington, D.C., or Boston, this site can help.

- *Vault Guide to Top Internships* by Samer Hamadeh, Mark Oldman, Marcy Lerner, and Laurie Pasiuk. Read this book for information on more than 750 top internships, including qualifications, pay, length of internship, and company background.

Still stumped? Here's a list of fields in which business majors can expect to find internships:

- Corporate accounting
- Banking
- Operations
- Marketing
- Retailing
- Management
- Consulting
- Web applications
- Corporate finance
- Sales
- Systems
- Public accounting

When looking for an internship, you'll want to keep the following points in mind:

◆ Don't leave your search until the last minute. The earlier you begin looking for an internship, the more likely you are to land a plum position. Likewise, don't miss the deadline when applying for an internship!

◆ Many people have the misconception that internships are for college juniors or seniors when in fact, many "first step" internships are available to all students. As noted by Tami Gove, President of InternWeb.com, these types of internships are typically unpaid and may be more clerical in nature. Although students with these types of internships may not work on the more challenging assignments, "they will be exposed to an organizational environment." This type of internship may also give students a leg up when seeking higher-level internships later in their studies.

◆ Learn as much as possible about any company where you're thinking of interning. This will help you determine whether you are a good fit.

◆ Treat your internship search just as you would a job search. Create a powerful résumé and cover letter, and practice your interviewing skills! Even more important, immediately follow up any interviews with a thank-you letter.

◆ Some interns find themselves acting as little more than glorified "gophers"; others enjoy a more nurturing professional experience as they learn the ins and outs of an industry. Before committing to any internship, make sure you understand what you can expect from it. Visit your college's career-counseling center for guidance, and see if you can nose out any fellow students who have interned at the site that interests you.

◆ If you're interested in a career in international business, consider interning abroad, either independently or through a study-abroad program that features an internship option. For information about overseas internships, visit your college's career-counseling center, or point your Web browser to www.studyabroad.com or www.internabroad.com. Alternatively, visit www.cie.uci.edu/iop/ internsh.html, hosted by UC Irvine's Center for International Education; there, you can find an extensive list of relevant Web links and study-abroad programs.

Participating in Campus Organizations

The more involved you are with campus-based organizations, the better you can demonstrate to potential employers your ability to manage your time. In addition, campus-based organizations afford you the unique opportunity to assume leadership roles that can mirror those you seek in the business world. Most colleges and universities offer a whopping number of campus organizations that can enhance the college experience of a business major, such as the following:

◆ *Social fraternities and sororities.* In addition to offering students an opportunity to increase their social sphere, these types of organizations offer students an unprecedented network upon graduation.

◆ *Athletic teams (varsity, club, and intramural).* Varsity athletes in high-profile sports often enjoy a high-profile status both during and after their college years, which can provide a real boon during any job hunt (assuming a student's athletic career ends upon graduation). But even participants in club and intramural sports can enjoy an edge over their less physically active college counterparts. Why? Sports teach people about excellence, discipline, and teamwork—all lessons that are relevant in business.

◆ *Business clubs and societies.* National business clubs and societies include Beta Gamma Sigma, which is the honor society that serves business programs accredited by the Association to Advance Collegiate Schools of Business (AACSB) International; Delta Sigma Pi, a co-ed professional business fraternity that boasts more than 250 chapters and 200,000 members nationwide; Alpha Kappa Psi, a co-ed fraternity dedicated to promoting and maintaining high standards of education, integrity, and leadership; and AIESEC, which is present in over 800 universities in 89 countries and territories and is, in its own words, "the international platform for young people to discover and develop their potential so as to have a positive impact in society." In addition to determining whether these clubs or societies are present at your school, you'll want to see what school-specific clubs and societies exist.

◆ *Diversity groups.* Whatever your ethnic origin, joining a diversity group is a great way to learn how to work with—and appreciate—all types of people.

◆ *Interest-based clubs and societies.* Whether you love billiards, bowling, bridge, the bassoon, or ballet, chances are your school has a club full of people who share your passion. Get involved!

If none of the clubs or organizations offered at your school capture your interest, you have a unique opportunity to demonstrate your leadership skills and entrepreneurial spirit by starting a club of your own.

In addition to participating in clubs and other campus organizations, you'll want to scour your campus for special opportunities, some paid and some volunteer, designed to give students a leg up in the working world. Here are a few examples:

◆ At the University of Colorado-Boulder, students involved in the Program Council learn the ins and outs of the music business by organizing on-campus gigs with big-name performers; visiting acts have included such legends as the Rolling Stones, the Dave Matthews Band, and Paul McCartney. Although the Program Council relies on a large cadre of volunteers, the core student staff—for example, the student director of the program—is paid.

◆ Georgetown University boasts Students of Georgetown Inc., a student-run corporation that employs more than 200 undergraduates in enterprises including a coffee joint, a used-book co-op, a video-rental store, a photo-development center, and a shipping and storage facility.

◆ Harvard, Stanford, and Columbia all feature book publishers for which students research, write, and market books.

◆ Students at University of Massachusetts-Amherst run, among other venues, a bike shop and a vegetarian restaurant.

◆ Nearly every school boasts a radio station and a television station. See if you can find work at yours in promotions or public relations.

◆ Odds are your college has a daily or weekly newspaper; you may be able to sign on as the paper's business manager, general manager, or marketing manager. Alternatively, see if you can write for the paper; you'll no doubt improve your writing and communication skills.

Whether these types of jobs put much-needed cash in your pocket or not, all provide you with the opportunity to learn the ins and outs of a business, including hiring help, contracting with vendors, developing and marketing new ideas, taking the initiative, showing leadership, and the like.

Maximizing Your Studies

In addition to any work experience you've gained during your years in school, prospective employers will be keenly interested in your academic record. Indeed, a strong academic record is an important way to differentiate yourself from rival candidates in your job search.

The key component of a strong academic record is your grade-point average (GPA). Beyond that, to stand out among a sea of applicants, you'll want to consider graduating with honors and obtaining a double major.

GPA

Your GPA offers employers their only reliable gauge of your performance in school. As such, you must approach your studies seriously, with the same discipline and focus you would a high-paying job. Here are some tips to help you earn the highest GPA possible:

◆ *Pinpoint your learning style.* For example, if you like to use visual association, imagery, written repetition, flash cards, or other similar devices, you're probably a visual learner. In contrast, if you use mnemonics or rhymes, or like to read your notes aloud, you're most likely an auditory learner. Reading/writing learners tend to rewrite ideas and principles in their own words; read and write their notes over and over; and rely on handouts, textbooks, and notes when studying; kinesthetic learners prefer more hands-on activities, such as field trips, to grasp key concepts.

◆ *Develop good listening habits.* Focus on the speaker and remain engaged in the discussion at hand. Remain intellectually curious; even the most "boring" subjects have some redeeming aspects, if you're willing to tease them out.

◆ *Take effective notes in class.* There are many different approaches to note-taking; decide which one works best for you. Whatever approach you choose, your notes should always include important points and key phrases; if your professor repeats something or writes it on the board, you should add it to your notes. If you find yourself falling behind in your note-taking, consider developing your own consistent form of shorthand (using abbreviations and the like) to speed things along.

◆ *Develop good study habits.* That means not just studying often, but studying well. Find a place to study that is free of distractions from music, TV, general noise, or interruptions, and that has good lighting, proper ventilation, and a comfortable place to sit. If you're a people person, look into joining or starting a study group. Many colleges and universities support academic skills centers designed to help students learn to study more effectively; if you find yourself having trouble making the grade, determine whether your school makes such a resource available to you.

◆ *Stay organized and manage your time.* Use a day-planner to write down class times, work times, assignments, and due dates and refer to it daily. Keep a running to-do list, and try to check off at least a few items each day. Take some time each Sunday to plan the week ahead, taking into account school, work, and personal obligations. Experts say you should study two to three hours per week for each credit hour taken. That means if you're taking 15 credit hours, you should study at least 30 hours a week.

◆ *Avoid procrastinating.* Begin working on any assignments you receive immediately, chipping away a bit at a time until they are complete.

◆ *Avoid cramming.* You should begin studying for a test or quiz well in advance, not the night before. Indeed, if you make it a habit to briefly review materials on a daily and/or weekly basis, you'll have a real leg up when mid-terms and finals roll around.

◆ *Take practice tests.* Many professors make available tests from previous years; if so, obtain a copy to see how you stack up before your exam day arrives.

◆ *Get help.* If you're having trouble grasping a concept or keeping up in class, seek guidance from the professor, another student, or a tutor.

◆ *Stay healthy.* Exercise and eat properly. Get adequate sleep. Don't smoke. Drink in moderation, if at all (assuming you're of legal age), and opt out of drugs altogether. Manage your stress to prevent it from overwhelming you. Take some time each day to do something that enriches your mind and spirit. Have some fun. Share your joys and troubles with your friends and family.

◆ *Keep it honest.* If you're looking for an abrupt and unhappy end to your college career, then by all means cheat or plagiarize. If, however, you'd like to graduate and obtain gainful employment afterward, then *don't.*

GRADUATING WITH HONORS: WRITING YOUR SENIOR THESIS

Graduating with honors is a great way to distinguish yourself among your fellow post-college job-seekers. At some schools, students who achieve a particular GPA—say, 3.5 or higher—graduate with honors automatically; other schools require eligible students (that is, students whose GPA is up to snuff) to write a senior thesis in order to graduate with honors.

If your school requires students to write a senior thesis in order to graduate with honors, consider doing so. Writing a senior thesis can be a great way to demonstrate your strengths both to your professors and to prospective employers. Writing a thesis is a lot of work, but it's a great opportunity to synthesize what you've learned during your course work. Here are some points to keep in mind when choosing and writing your senior thesis:

◆ Choose a thesis topic that relates to the field you want to enter during your career. For example, if your dream is to work in investment banking, your thesis should relate to that field in some way. This gives you a chance to both learn more about that field and demonstrate what you know.

◆ Choose a thesis topic that enables you to explore an issue that has not yet been resolved. This is your *governing question*. For example, your governing question might be "Why is health care so expensive in the United States?" Realize, though, that you don't need to answer your governing question; indeed, you may not be able to. Simply addressing the complexity of it may be adequate.

◆ Don't be surprised if your thesis takes some unexpected turns. You may find during the course of your research and writing that the answer—or your views about—your governing question may be different from what you thought. Be open to this.

DOUBLE MAJOR/DOUBLE DEGREE

If you know what industry you want to enter with your business major, consider obtaining a double major (that is, one degree with two majors) or double degree (two separate degrees) to better your chances.

For example, if you are certain you want to work in the technology sector, a business degree coupled with a degree in computer science will almost certainly give you an edge. Likewise, if you know you want to work in international business, obtaining a second major in a foreign language may prove helpful.

Of course, the downside is that in order to graduate with a double major or double degree, you must complete the course work of both— no easy feat. Whether you are eligible for a double major or a double degree typically depends on the number of credits you were required to complete in order to complete the required course work. For example, students might be awarded one bachelor's degree with two majors if the required accumulated credits range from 180 to 224. A double degree, on the other hand, might be awarded if 225 or more credits are required. Double degrees are also typically awarded if the majors are in two different colleges, or if one major yields a B.A. while the other yields a B.S.

Volunteering

It's a sad fact: There just aren't enough paid internships available for college students. If you fail to garner an internship, or if you just want to make a difference in your community, consider volunteering as a way to boost your résumé—and your soul. When you do volunteer work that pertains to your course work—called "career volunteering"—everybody wins. As a business major, you'll want to look for volunteering opportunities that enable you to confer your newfound business knowledge to a needy organization; this enables you to make an even bigger impact for good. You obtain real-world experience, broaden your network, and help others, all in one fell swoop. In addition, you may even be able to obtain academic "service-learning" credits.

Here are some great places to start looking for career volunteer opportunities in your area:

◆ *Your school's career or volunteer center.* Many colleges and universities help match students with volunteer opportunities that are related to their major. If your school does, look there first.

◆ *Your local United Way.* Part of a national network of giving, each United Way nationwide aims to address critical local issues. At the very least, your local United Way may be able to point you in the right direction.

◆ *Local websites.* The website for your city or town may list volunteer opportunities in your community; check it out.

◆ *Project Sledgehammer (www.projectsledgehammer.org).* In its own words, this organization empowers students "to connect to a deeper passion and purpose in order to discover their life's work and lead the next generation." On its website you'll find a free database with more than 750 career volunteering opportunities (at last count).

◆ *VolunteerMatch (www.volunteermatch.org).* This nonprofit organization's website is dedicated to helping everyone find great places to volunteer. Simply enter your zip code, and VolunteerMatch returns a list of local volunteer opportunities.

◆ *Idealist.org (www.idealist.org).* A project of Action Without Borders, idealist.org enables you to search or browse 40,000 nonprofit and community organizations in 165 countries. You'll also find jobs and internships at nonprofits listed here.

## Chapter 4

Attending Graduate School

Meet Ian. He's smart and well educated, having received a BS in Kinesiology at the University of Colorado and an MS in Electrical Engineering from the same institution. Still, he found himself frustrated at his IT job, unable to make the leap from being the guy who implemented decisions made by others to being the guy who called the shots. For Ian, returning to school to obtain his Masters in Business Administration (MBA) was the natural choice. Currently, although he is one semester shy of wrapping up his studies, Ian has already found a better job as the Assistant Director of Business and Technology with the Indiana University Medical School's Continuing Medical Education Department.

Are you like Ian? Have you found yourself dead-ended at the far reaches of your career path? If so, then an MBA might be the answer for you, too. This chapter is designed to help you decide whether an MBA is right for you, determine how obtaining an MBA can help you with your job search, discover what sort of undergraduate background and grades are required, find out how to obtain excellent letters of recommendation from professors and other sources, figure out how to pay for your schooling, and estimate how much time you can expect to devote to your studies. You'll also find a list of the top MBA programs in the nation.

Is an MBA Right for You?

First the bad news: To obtain an MBA at a top school, you can expect to spend nearly $80,000 in tuition alone over a two-year period—on top of giving up your salary in order to attend full time. Of course, attending part time is an option with some programs, but that's no picnic. After working 40+ hours, the last thing most people want to do is hunker down in a lecture hall two evenings a week, not to mention study all weekend—for three years.

Now, for the points in the plus column: Most MBA grads command high salaries, sometimes even six figures (not counting bonuses), right out of school. Moreover, MBAs generally land jobs that put them in the driver's seat.

So how do you decide whether an MBA is right for you? Ask yourself two questions:

1. What are my career goals?

2. Will business school help me meet those goals?

For example, if your goal is to enter the field of investment banking or consulting, then an MBA is practically a requirement. And the credibility that an MBA provides can be useful in any number of job scenarios. But some fields may view a certain period of relevant work experience as equally valuable.

If you're looking for a complete change in career—for example, if you're an engineer who has exhausted your ability to move forward on your current career path, and wish to move to management—then an MBA can be instrumental in helping you make the switch.

Top MBA Programs in the United States

Just which schools offer the top MBA programs in the United States? Interestingly, they're not always the schools whose undergraduate programs excel—although you will find some crossover (Penn's Wharton School, MIT's Sloan School of Management, and the University of Michigan's Ross School of Business come to mind). *Business Week* ranks the best full-time MBA programs every two years; its 2004 rankings are as follows:

1. Northwestern University Kellogg School of Management
2. University of Chicago Graduate School of Business
3. University of Pennsylvania Wharton School
4. Stanford Graduate School of Business
5. Harvard Business School
6. University of Michigan Ross School of Business
7. Cornell University S.C. Johnson School of Management
8. Columbia Business School
9. MIT Sloan School of Management
10. Dartmouth College Tuck School of Business

NORTHWESTERN UNIVERSITY KELLOGG SCHOOL OF MANAGEMENT

www.kellogg.northwestern.edu

Located 20 minutes from Chicago, Northwestern University's Kellogg School of Management boasts the nation's top-rated MBA program. Noted for its culture and esprit de corps, not to mention its outstanding professors, administrators, and students, Kellogg had a selectivity rate of 23 percent in 2004. The school offers 23 concentrations varying from accounting to organizational behavior to transportation. An accelerated one-year program is available.

Northwestern University Kellogg School of Management MBA Program Specs (2004–05)*			
Full-Time Students	*Part-Time Students*	*Length of Full-Time Program*	*Total Cost (Not Annual)*
1,250	1,350	22 months	$72,740

*as reported by *Business Week*

University of Chicago Graduate School of Business MBA Program Specs (2004–05)*			
Full-Time Students	*Part-Time Students*	*Length of Full-Time Program*	*Total Cost (Not Annual)*
1,088	1,433	21 months	$65,912

*as reported by *Business Week*

UNIVERSITY OF CHICAGO GRADUATE SCHOOL OF BUSINESS

http://chicagogsb.edu

The University of Chicago's Graduate School of Business's MBA program boasts 13 areas of study, from analytic finance to entrepreneurship. At 23 percent, the University of Chicago's selectivity rate mirrors that of Northwestern's. Recently, the University of Chicago Graduate School of Business unveiled its Hyde Park Center, featuring state-of-the-art technology for data, video, audio, and more, and representing a $12-million investment in the school's future.

UNIVERSITY OF PENNSYLVANIA WHARTON SCHOOL

http://mba.wharton.upenn.edu/mba

The University of Pennsylvania's Wharton School, arguably the most represented and most powerful MBA program on Wall Street, is highly selective, accepting only 16 percent of applicants in 2004. Featuring 17 concentrations, including sports business, graduates of the Wharton School enjoy high starting salaries, with a median starting base salary of $99,000 in 2004. Enjoy learning at the school's new Huntsman building, featuring fully wired classrooms and study rooms.

University of Pennsylvania Wharton School MBA Program Specs (2004–05)*			
Full-Time Students	*Part-Time Students*	*Length of Full-Time Program*	*Total Cost (Not Annual)*
1,671	0	18 months	$72,771 (2003)

*as reported by *Business Week*

Stanford Graduate School of Business MBA Program Specs (2004–05)*			
Full-Time Students	Part-Time Students	Length of Full-Time Program	Total Cost (Not Annual)
754	0	21 months	$75,996

*as reported by *Business Week*

STANFORD GRADUATE SCHOOL OF BUSINESS
www-gsb.stanford.edu

Among the most selective MBA programs in the nation, Stanford, located in northern California, accepted only 10 percent of applicants in 2004, 9 percent in 2003, and 8 percent in 2002. Enrolled students concentrate on one of three courses of study—general management, global management, or public management—and can opt to focus their studies in one of a number of areas, including corporate social responsibility, entrepreneurship, finance, organizational behavior, and strategy. Graduates of the program enjoy high starting salaries, averaging $100,600 in 2004 (excluding bonuses). If you're looking to pursue a career on the West Coast, Stanford may well be the place for you.

HARVARD BUSINESS SCHOOL
www.hbs.edu

If you believe "who you know" trumps "what you know," then there's no better place than Harvard Business School, nestled in the heart of Cambridge, Massachusetts. With roughly 40,000 living alumni and 111

Harvard Business School MBA Program Specs (2004–05)*			
Full-Time Students	Part-Time Students	Length of Full-Time Program	Total Cost (Not Annual)
1,796	0	22 months	$78,200

*as reported by *Business Week*

MBA clubs in 49 countries, networking opportunities abound. And when it comes to impressing others, the Harvard name is second to none.

UNIVERSITY OF MICHIGAN ROSS SCHOOL OF BUSINESS
www.bus.umich.edu

If you're attending business school with a particular career path in mind—say, in health care administration or portfolio management—then the University of Michigan's Ross School of Business can almost certainly accommodate your specific needs. At the Ross School of Business, students can select one of 29 concentrations in fields ranging from accounting to technology, and including a few concentrations not found in most other top MBA schools, such as business history. In addition, Michigan is known for having one of the best dual-degree programs in the nation.

University of Michigan Ross School of Business MBA Program Specs (2004–05)*			
Full-Time Students	**Part-Time Students**	**Length of Full-Time Program**	**Total Cost (Not Annual)**
841	952	20 months	$65,376 (resident); $75,376 (nonresident)

*as reported by *Business Week*

CORNELL UNIVERSITY S.C. JOHNSON SCHOOL OF MANAGEMENT
www.johnson.cornell.edu

Among the top-10 schools, Cornell University's S.C. Johnson School of Management was among the most generous to prospective students, accepting 36 percent of applicants for the 2004–05 academic year and offering 58 full-tuition scholarships. The school's secluded location (it's tucked away in Ithaca, New York, in the heart of the Finger Lakes region, amidst farmland, vineyards, and state parks) and small class sizes offer yet another draw. And unlike many other top-tier programs,

Cornell University S.C. Johnson School of Management MBA Program Specs (2004–05)*			
Full-Time Students	Part-Time Students	Length of Full-Time Program	Total Cost (Not Annual)
544	0	21 months	$71,320

*as reported by *Business Week*

Cornell offers a 12-month option for students with advanced degrees (Masters or higher) in science or engineering.

COLUMBIA BUSINESS SCHOOL
www.gsb.columbia.edu

If you're looking for easy access to internships, part-time employment, corporate recruiters, and top-level executives, then Columbia is the place to be. Located in Manhattan, the Columbia School of Business offers MBA students the unique ability to study in a city where nearly every major industry and corporation houses either its headquarters or a major facility. And if you're looking to expedite your studies, you can take advantage of Columbia's accelerated 16-month program, in which students forego a summer internship.

Columbia Business School MBA Program Specs (2004–05)*			
Full-Time Students	Part-Time Students	Length of Full-Time Program	Total Cost (Not Annual)
1,196	0	20 months	$72,590

*as reported by *Business Week*

MIT SLOAN SCHOOL OF MANAGEMENT
http://mitsloan.mit.edu/mba

If you come from a technical background, you may well find a home at MIT's Sloan School of Management, perched across the river from the

MIT Sloan School of Management MBA Program Specs (2004–05)*			
Full-Time Students	**Part-Time Students**	**Length of Full-Time Program**	**Total Cost (Not Annual)**
781	776	18 months	$37,050

*as reported by *Business Week*

Harvard campus, thanks to the MBA program's focus on innovation, entrepreneurship, and technology.

DARTMOUTH COLLEGE TUCK SCHOOL OF BUSINESS

www.tuck.dartmouth.edu

A small school in a small town in New Hampshire, Dartmouth College's Tuck School of Business offers an unrivalled sense of community with your fellow students. As one student quoted in *Business Week* observed, "With only 240 classmates in a small town in the middle of nowhere, you really become tight and develop lifelong friendships and hone your teamwork skills." In addition, Tuck is noted for its supportive alumni base and caring faculty and staff.

Dartmouth College Tuck School of Business MBA Program Specs (2004–05)*			
Full-Time Students	**Part-Time Students**	**Length of Full-Time Program**	**Total Cost (Not Annual)**
500	0	21 months	$77,715

*as reported by *Business Week*

Evaluating Other Schools

If, for whatever reason, the schools listed here don't meet your needs—perhaps you are obligated to stay close to home, or your finances won't permit the tuition assessed by these institutions—don't fret. Just because a school isn't in the top 10 or even the top 20 doesn't mean you can't leverage your education there to achieve your goals. In addition, certain MBA programs may excel at a particular discipline but not be terribly distinguished overall. The bottom line? Don't be discouraged if your circumstances prevent you from attending one of the schools listed here. When you're armed with an MBA from *any* accredited, reputable institution, the sky is the limit.

What Sort of Time Is Required?

If you pursue your MBA as a full-time student, you can anticipate spending anywhere from 18 to 22 months completing the program, often including a summer internship. Prospective part-time students should expect to spend an additional year enrolled.

Admissions Considerations

One frustrating aspect of applying to an MBA program is the general lack of a quantitative formula for admission. That is, the admissions process is subjective and differs from program to program. That said, a few important consistent criteria can be noted:

- ◆ MBA programs typically accept students of all majors—from architecture to zoology and everything in between. Candidates who have completed an undergraduate curriculum that is well rounded and challenging often have a leg up over their highly specialized undergraduate counterparts. Some MBA programs do require applicants to have completed certain prerequisite courses before applying, however; check with your prospective schools for more details.

- ◆ More important than one's major are his or her grades, GMAT test scores (see "Test Scores" below), and general college achievements (refer to Chapter 3 for more information).

- ◆ Many MBA programs take into consideration any work experience you've obtained since completing your undergraduate studies.

- ◆ Other factors considered by admissions officers include the essay and letters of recommendation.

GRADES

Although undergraduate grades play a significant role in one's eligibility for most MBA programs, almost no programs require a minimum GPA. You'll find that the average undergraduate GPA for students at the more competitive programs, however, tends to run fairly high. The table below outlines the average undergraduate GPAs for students in *Business Week's* top-10 MBA programs, in cases where such information was available.

TEST SCORES

Before you apply for any MBA program, you must take the Graduate Management Admission Test (GMAT), which is a standardized test that consists of math, verbal, and writing sections. (Most likely, you'll want to allow yourself several months to study for this test either independently or by enrolling in a test-prep course.)

The table on p. 57 outlines the minimum (if applicable) and average GMAT scores of students enrolled in the nation's top-10 MBA programs (as compiled by *Business Week*). You'll also find information about Test of English as a Foreign Language (TOEFL) scores here, which some

Undergraduate GPA Stats (2004)		
School	*Minimum GPA*	*Average GPA*
Northwestern	None	N/A*
Chicago	None	3.4 (class entering in 2002)
Wharton	None	3.5
Stanford	None	N/A*
Harvard	None	N/A*
Michigan	None	3.3 to 3.5
Cornell	N/A*	N/A*
Columbia	N/A*	3.0 to 3.9 (class entering in 2003)
MIT	N/A*	N/A*
Dartmouth	N/A*	N/A*

*information not available

Test Score Information (2004)

School	GMAT Minimum	GMAT Average	TOEFL Average	TOEFL Minimum
Northwestern	None	700	649	N/A*
Chicago	None	695	N/A*	600
Wharton	None	N/A*	N/A*	N/A*
Stanford	None	711	657	600
Harvard	None	707	656	607
Michigan	None	692	645	600
Cornell	N/A*	673	643	600
Columbia	N/A*	706	N/A*	N/A*
MIT	None	697	N/A*	N/A*
Dartmouth	None	704	648	N/A*

*information not available

schools require if you are an ESL (English as a Second Language) student. If you plan to apply at a school not on this list, comb that school's website to see if similar information is posted there.

WORK EXPERIENCE

MBA programs value a candidate's work experience a great deal. As noted on the Northwestern University Kellogg School of Management website, "[The Admissions Committee] highly values full-time professional experience. Work experience adds to maturity and career- and self-awareness, which contribute to a student's success." Indeed, the Kellogg School of Business recommends that prospective students have at least two years of full-time work experience; on average, enrolled students at that school have approximately five years under their belts.

As noted on the University of Chicago Graduate School of Business website, however, *quality* of work experience—in addition to quantity— is important. When applying to an MBA program, make it a point to highlight skills you've developed in the work force, contributions you've made to your place of employment, and any leadership roles you've assumed during your tenure there.

Work Experience (2004)*

School	Average Work Experience
Northwestern	62 months
Chicago	59 months
Wharton	N/A**
Stanford	48 months
Harvard	53 months
Michigan	62 months
Cornell	60 months
Columbia	59 months
MIT	64 months
Dartmouth	61 months

*as reported by *Business Week*   **information not available

That said, most schools do not have a requirement for a *minimum* number of years of work experience. If you plan to enroll in an MBA program immediately after completing your undergraduate studies, you'll want to ensure you make the most of your undergraduate experience to enhance the likelihood of acceptance into an MBA program (refer to Chapter 3 for more information). Be aware, however, that not only does some degree of full-time work experience increase a candidate's likelihood of being accepted into an MBA program, but it also gives enrolled MBA students a frame of reference that enhances learning.

The table above outlines the average work experience for students in the incoming class of 2004 at *Business Week*'s top-10 MBA programs.

WRITING YOUR ESSAYS

Describe a significant change that you brought about in an organization and its impact on your development as a leader.

What are your three most substantial accomplishments, and why do you view them as such?

Provide a candid assessment of your strengths and weaknesses.

How do you define success?

These musings, from the Harvard Business School MBA application, are just a few examples of essay topics you may be required to address. How can you make your responses rise above the fray? Here are a few points to consider:

♦ Convey your best self without sounding conceited. Even as you try to impress your reader with your accomplishments and abilities, you must remain likable. As the folks at GMAT MBA Prep put it, "As a rule, if anything you write sounds like something Napolean would say, then it should be edited."

♦ Remember that the person reading your essays has probably been roped into reading hundreds more over the course of several days. Show him or her some mercy by ensuring that your essay is well within the word limit.

♦ Ask someone to proofread your essay. The presence of typos, spelling errors, and/or grammatical mistakes will make you look careless and unprofessional.

♦ Use the proper tone. That means avoiding overblown business-speak while at the same time eschewing overly casual language. Take special care to omit clichés and other overused phrases, such as "think outside the box."

OBTAINING LETTERS OF RECOMMENDATION

When it comes to obtaining letters of recommendation, remember these key points:

♦ Choose the right person to write the letter. This might be a favorite professor or your college advisor, a boss with whom you established a positive connection, a family friend who holds a high-ranking position of some sort, or a friend who has successfully completed an MBA program. Ask your letter-writing candidates personally to complete the favor, and volunteer to meet with them at a time of their choosing. And of course, when the task is complete, remember to thank your letter-writers!

♦ Be certain to give any recommenders adequate time to write a strong letter of recommendation. To expedite matters, consider supplying recommenders a checklist about yourself. Ajeet Khurana, the Business Major guide on About.com, suggests you include information about where you went to college, your GPA, your major, any extracurricular activities you enjoyed, any work experience you've had, volunteer work you've performed, and your career goals. Khurana also urges you to provide for the letter-writer information about the institution to which the letter should be sent (including the mailing address), specific instructions (if any), and any applicable deadlines.

◆ For maximum credibility, forfeit your right to read the letter before it is sent.

Paying for Your MBA

As mentioned previously, obtaining an MBA at a top school can run upwards of $80,000. And if you opt to attend full time, that means you forego whatever salary you may earn at your current job. So short of inheriting a bundle from a distant relative, how does one pay for such an endeavor?

Financing Your MBA Education*			
School	Financial Aid Available?	Scholarships Available?	Business School Endowment
Northwestern	Yes	Yes	$433,000,000
Chicago	Yes	Yes	$221,400,000
Wharton	Yes	Yes	$435,500,000
Stanford	Yes	Yes	$587,000,000
Harvard	Yes	Yes	$1,800,000,000
Michigan	Yes	Yes	$246,200,000
Cornell	Yes	Yes	$112,000,000
Columbia	Yes	Yes	$260,000,000
MIT	Yes	Yes	$413,000,000
Dartmouth	Yes	Yes	$168,000,000

*as reported by *Business Week*

Fortunately, just about every MBA program out there offers some sort of financial aid, usually through a dedicated office in the school itself. Scholarships may also be available. The preceding table outlines financing options available at the nation's top-10 MBA schools (as compiled by *Business Week*), as well as the size of each school's endowment (odds are, the larger the endowment, the more scholarship opportunities you'll find available to you).

## Chapter 5

Career Options for the Business Major

A business major instills in the eager student several skills and abilities that transfer well to any number of jobs in any number of industries: oral- and written-communication skills, listening skills, leadership skills, organizational skills, and analytical skills—not to mention the ability to persuade others to your viewpoint, generate new ideas, think critically, and manage your time. All these, plus the work ethic and self-discipline you're sure to develop during the course of your studies, will serve you well upon graduation.

Armed with your business major, you have countless career opportunities available to you. Of course, there are jobs in the obvious fields, which tend to mirror the study concentrations offered by many business programs:

◆ Accounting

◆ Finance

◆ Management

◆ Marketing

◆ Operations

The nice thing about being a business major, though, is that you can apply your skills to nearly any field. Do you have a passion for flying?

Then you might enjoy working in the accounting department of your local airport. Do you love to paint? Armed with your business degree, you're primed to keep the books for your favorite art gallery. And of course, a business major goes a long way toward preparing you for entrepreneurial endeavors. This chapter is designed to help you realize just what types of jobs exist for people with undergraduate degrees in business.

Accounting Jobs for Business Majors

If you earned your BBA or BSBA with a concentration in accounting, you're primed to enter the work force in any one of the following accounting career paths:

◆ *Auditing.* This involves checking accounting ledgers and financial statements both within corporations and government offices to ensure their accuracy. Entry-level jobs in this career path include Auditor, Internal Auditor, and Staff Auditor.

◆ *Budget analysis.* If you're interested in developing and managing the financial plan of an organization, be it in government or private industry, then budget analysis may be the field for you. Entry-level jobs in this career path include Budget Analyst.

◆ *Financial accounting.* This type of work requires a solid under-standing of both finance and accounting, because it involves preparing financial statements, and making finance-related deci-sions and long-term financial projections. Entry-level jobs in this career path include Financial Consultant, Financial Accountant, Financial Specialist, and Financial Analyst.

◆ *Management accounting.* Although workers in this field, frequently referred to as "bean counters," have historically been viewed in a negative light, this assessment is changing. These days, management accountants work with marketing and finance departments to establish financial strategies. Entry-level jobs in this career path include Cost Accountant, Staff Accountant, and Project Accountant.

Major Employers in the Field

Accounting jobs can typically be found in the following types of organizations:

- *Public accounting firms.* These include Accenture, Coopers & Lybrand, Deloitte Touche, Ernst & Young, KPMG Peat Marwick, and Price Waterhouse.

- *Government.* This includes government offices at the local, state, and federal levels.

- *Corporations.* Most corporations have an accounting group responsible for preparing financial statements, tracking costs, and handling other accounting-related issues.

Abilities/Additional Training Needed

To be successful in accounting, you'll of course need a firm understanding of accounting procedures and solid analytical skills. Because the industry is becoming increasingly technological in nature, computer skills are a must. In addition, because you'll most likely start your career in accounting as a junior member of a team, you should understand how to work effectively with others. Finally, be aware of recent trends that show accountants broadening their skill sets to include legal knowledge, sales abilities, and foreign-language skills.

If you find that your BBA or BSBA major with a concentration in accounting (or, in some cases, finance) doesn't afford you the type of accounting job you want, consider obtaining your Certified Public Accountant (CPA) certification.

Salary

According to Salary.com (which reviews available, applicable market pay data to determine a job's market value), the median salary for a Level I Accounting job—that is, a job that requires workers to prepare balance sheets, profit and loss statements, and other financial reports—is $38,107. Note that various factors affect the salary of a job in this field, including location, size of organization, and the like.

Finance Jobs for Business Majors

If you earned your BBA or BSBA with a concentration in finance, you're well prepared for an entry-level position in any one of the following finance-related fields:

◆ *Investment banking.* This field covers a wide range of financial activities, including aiding in the issue and purchase of securities, managing financial assets, and providing financial advice. Entry-level jobs in investment banking include Junior Analyst and Research Associate.

◆ *Commercial banking.* Commercial banks serve a wide range of customers, from individuals to small businesses to large corporations and other organizations. It follows, then, that employment opportunities in commercial banks are likewise broad, from positions at local branches to jobs geared toward international finance. Indeed, commercial banks employ far more workers than any other sector of the financial-services industry. Entry-level positions in this field include Bank Teller, Bank Administrator, and Loan Officer.

◆ *Financial planning.* If you enjoy helping others achieve their dreams, you may opt for a career as a financial planner. As a financial planner, you help others plan for retirement, put their children through college, and fulfill other life ambitions such as purchasing a vacation home or yacht. Entry-level positions in this field include Associate Financial Planner.

◆ *Insurance.* The mission of the trillion-dollar insurance industry, which employs more than 2.5 million workers in the United States, is to help individuals and businesses choose the best insurance policies for protecting them against catastrophic losses. Entry-level jobs in this industry for candidates possessing a BBA or BSBA include Underwriter, Sales Representative, Asset Manager, Customer Service Representative, and Actuary.

◆ *Corporate finance.* Whether working for a global company or a local standout, business graduates who enter the field of corporate finance can expect to help their company find cash to run and grow the business and plan for its financial future. One benefit of working in corporate finance is that these jobs tend to be stable—that is, because the position takes a long-term view, bumps in the short term tend not to affect your employed status. Entry-level positions in this field include Junior Financial Analyst and Corporate Finance and Restructuring Associate.

◆ *Money management.* If your dream is to analyze market trends and buy stocks and bonds for clients accordingly, then money management is the field for you. Unfortunately, however, unlike fields such as banking and insurance, getting started in the money-management game can be difficult. If you find this door shut to you upon graduating with your BBA or BSBA, consider starting your career with a bank trust department, an insurance company, a state or local pension fund, or in investment banking.

◆ *Real estate.* More than one-third of the world's wealth lies in real estate, which acts as collateral for mortgages and other financial assets. An industry that employs more than five million people in the United States alone—not including professionals involved in corporate real estate or in real-estate lending—real estate may well be the field for you. Entry-level jobs in real estate for candidates who have earned a BBA or BSBA include Real Estate Financial Analyst, Real Estate Broker, Corporate Real Estate Manager, and Real Estate Securities Analyst.

Major Employers in the Field

The major employers in the finance field vary by discipline. The following sections outline the big hitters:

◆ *Investment banking.* These include Merrill Lynch, Salomon Smith Barney, Morgan Stanley Dean Witter, and Goldman Sachs.

◆ *Commercial banking.* These include Bank One Corp., Bank of America Corp., Citigroup, KeyCorp, and Wachovia Corporation.

◆ *Financial planning.* These include CIGNA, Paine Webber, and Merrill Lynch.

- *Insurance.* These include AFLAC, The Allstate Corporation, CIGNA, Metropolitan Life Insurance Company, The State Farm Insurance Companies, and The Progressive Corporation.

- *Corporate finance.* Candidates for positions in corporate finance may find work in any number of corporations in industries of all types.

- *Money management.* These include Merrill Lynch Asset Management, Fidelity, Charles Schwab, State Street Global Advisors, and Morgan Stanley Dean Witter.

- *Real estate.* These include Trammell Crow, Lincoln Property, CB Richard Ellis, Cushman and Wakefield Worldwide, Jones Lang LaSalle, and Grubb & Ellis.

Abilities/Additional Training Needed

Required abilities and additional training differ depending on which finance discipline you choose. Regardless of which sub-field you choose, you'll need a keen understanding of numbers, of market forces, and of the market itself. The ability to work in teams will also serve you well, especially at the outset of your career. If you're interested in financial planning, consider obtaining your Certified Financial Planner (CFP) designation; if money management is your game, you'll want to obtain your Certified Financial Analyst (CFA) designation instead.

Salary

Your salary in finance can vary widely, depending on which discipline you choose—especially after you've been in the field for a few years. Note also that various other factors affect the salary of a job in this field, including location and size of the organization. For example, according to Salary.com (which reviews available, applicable market pay data to determine a job's market value), the median salary for a bank teller in Indianapolis is $20,851; a Level I Financial Analyst in Manhattan, on the other hand, can expect to pull a median salary of $57,321.

Management Jobs for Business Majors

If your business studies focused on management, your career options upon graduation are not limited primarily to a single industry, unlike students who choose to focus on, say, accounting or finance. Graduates with a BBA or BSBA with a concentration in management will find themselves especially prepared to enter a company, whatever the industry, as a management trainee. Other similar graduates may opt to enter the field of management consulting.

Major Employers in the Field

As mentioned previously, opportunities for BBA/BSBA with a focus in management span nearly every industry, from broadcast entertainment to health care to insurance to manufacturing to retail to software and beyond. As such, there is no "major employer" in this field per se. As for jobs in management consulting, major employers include the following:

- ◆ AT Kearney

- ◆ Bain & Company

- ◆ Booz Allen Hamilton

- ◆ Capgemini

Abilities/Additional Training Needed

Required abilities and additional training will differ depending on whether you wish to become a management consultant or simply work in management in a particular industry. In general, however, an understanding of industry-specific best business practices and management concepts will serve you well, as will an ability to work with all kinds of people.

Salary

Just as the types of jobs available to graduates with a BBA/BSBA and a focus in management vary, so, too, do the salaries. For example, according to Salary.com (which reviews available, applicable market pay data to determine a job's market value), a Branch Management Trainee in

Denver can expect to earn a median salary of $33,351; meanwhile, Monster.com's Salary Wizard suggests that the median salary of a Business Development Associate in San Francisco is $57,382.

Marketing Jobs for Business Majors

Armed with your BBA/BSBA with a concentration in marketing, you're poised to enter any one of the following main marketing fields:

◆ *Brand management/product management.* Specialists in this field are responsible for developing and executing programs, such as ad campaigns, designed to increase brand and/or product identity. In general, those interested in entering the field of brand/product management begin their careers in sales, communications, or advertising.

◆ *Advertising.* Those involved in advertising develop ad campaigns (print, radio, television, Web, and so on) to increase public awareness about a product, brand, or idea. Entry-level jobs in this field include Junior Art Director and Junior Copywriter.

◆ *Market research.* Professionals in this discipline gather and analyze data about the sale of goods and services to consumers. Entry-level jobs in this field include Research Assistant and Marketing Interviewer.

◆ *Public relations.* Those involved in public relations are charged with cultivating and maintaining a favorable public image for a company, product, brand, and the like. Many in public relations work in a freelance capacity, although numerous PR firms do exist.

Major Employers in the Field

Marketing is not unlike management in that it affords careers in any number of industries in addition to jobs in consulting firms. Leading marketing consulting firms in various marketing fields follow. In addition, you'll find a listing of the top brands and the companies that own them, which may prove useful to you if your interest is in brand/product management.

◆ *Advertising.* These include Foote Cone & Belding, J. Walter Thompson, Leo Burnett, BBDO Worldwide, Saatchi & Saatchi, and Ogilvy.

◆ *Market research.* These include Forrester Research, Frost & Sullivan, Gartner Group, and Yankee Group.

◆ *Public relations.* These include Burson-Marsteller, Hill and Knowlton, Edelman Public Relations Worldwide, Fleishman-Hillard, Ketchum Communications, and Rowland Worldwide.

◆ *Top brands.* These include Coca-Cola, owned by Coca-Cola Co.; IBM, owned by IBM; Microsoft, owned by Microsoft; Kodak, owned by Eastman Kodak Company; Budweiser, owned by Anheuser-Busch; Nestle, owned by Nestle USA Inc.; and McDonald's, owned by McDonald's Corporation.

Abilities/Additional Training Needed

In marketing, the ability to think creatively is always a plus, as is a strong sense of the cultural forces that affect people's purchasing decisions. Certain entry-level positions in marketing, such as in market research and brand management, require an MBA.

Salary

Salaries for graduates with a BBA/BSBA who enter into the marketing field vary by discipline and location. For example, according to www.careers-in-marketing.com, a Junior Art Director or Junior Copywriter at Leo Burnett in Chicago can expect to earn from $18,000 to $25,000. The same site quotes a salary of $17,000 and up for freelance Public Relations professionals.

Jobs for Business Majors in Operations

If you've graduated with a BBA or BSBA in business with a concentration in operations, your ideal job will be one that involves managing production/operations systems that produce goods or services. Equipped with your education, you are prepared to assume a first-level line or staff position in production or operations for a manufacturing, service, or government organization. According to the U.S. Department of Labor, common entry-level positions in this field include Management Trainee, Management Analyst, and Industrial Production Manager.

Major Employers in the Field

Operations jobs can be found wherever manufacturing is a prevalent industry; there are no "major employers" per se. According to the U.S. Department of Labor, key industries in the field include the following:

◆ Semiconductor and other electronic component manufacturing

◆ Motor vehicle parts manufacturing

◆ Plastics products manufacturing

◆ Printing and related support activities

Abilities/Additional Training Needed

Those who work in operations will generally need both an understanding of operations and strong people skills in order to analyze business trends and manage others. To enter higher-level positions in this field, such as Operations Research Analyst, an MBA may be required.

Salary

Salaries in operations-related positions vary widely and depend on various factors, such as type of industry and size and location of firm. In its data with regard to Management Analysts, the U.S. Department of Labor cites the median salary for entry-level consultants as $61,496; the California Employment Development Department puts the median wage of Management Trainees at $25.52 per hour. The U.S. Department of Labor does not provide salary statistics for entry-level Industrial Production Managers, but does note that the median salary for all Industrial Production Managers was $67,320 in 2002, with the lowest 10 percent earning roughly $38,980.

Unusual Career Paths for the Business Major

The fact is, equipped with a business major, you are uniquely prepared to embark on any number of career paths—not just those listed here. As mentioned earlier in this chapter, one strategy you might employ in order to choose your career is to assess your passions. A little soul searching can help you pick just the right job—and life—for you.

For example, do you love to sail? Then see whether any sailboat manufacturers are looking for help marketing their wares. Is wine your bag? Odds are there's a vineyard somewhere looking for help running its operations. Whether your interest lies in reading or beading, rowing or mowing, your perfect job may be just a phone call away.

If you're an activist at heart, don't overlook job opportunities at non-profit organizations, which comprise a large sector of economic activity. In addition to enabling you to make a real difference for a cause dear to your heart, working for a nonprofit is a great way to wrangle experience in many business disciplines early in your career. Due to budget constraints, many nonprofits simply can't afford to hire one person to handle marketing, another to keep the books, and a third to interface with potential donors; that means you may well have a hand in each area yourself. Although your salary probably won't match that of your investment-banking business brethren, think of what you'll learn!

Entrepreneurial Endeavors

If you long to be your own boss, a business major can serve you well. *Entrepreneur Magazine* breaks down the process of starting your own business into three major steps:

1. *Understand the business.* This involves researching your industry, hooking up with any related organizations, and networking with others in the field. In particular, you'll want to find out what types of material goods you need to run the business, what kinds of people you need to hire, what types of expenses you can expect to incur, where you're likely to snare your income, common pitfalls, and the like.

2. *Prepare a business plan.* This can help you more precisely determine your potential expenses and income.

3. *Make it happen.* Specifically, gather the people and funds you need, rent space, and buy the supplies you need.

People equipped with a business major already have many of the tools needed to complete these three steps. You have the skills to analyze an industry. You know how to prepare a business plan. You have access to people (your classmates, for starters) and you know where to go for funds (banks, venture capitalists, and so forth). So get started!

## Chapter 6

Breaking into the Job Market

After four (or five or six) long years of college, you're ready to fly the coop, business degree in hand. For most people, that means finding their first real job. This chapter is designed to help college students, recent grads, or anyone interested in changing careers find—and land—a great job.

You should approach your job search just as you would any, er, *job*—with organization, focus, and discipline. Here are some tips to make your search easier:

◆ Experts suggest job seekers spend at least two hours daily, six days a week, engaged in job-hunt activities—finding job postings, gathering contacts, sending résumés and cover letters, interviewing, and the like. Of course, this is merely a suggestion; if your schedule does not permit this, develop a plan that works for you—and stick with it. The point is to develop a job-hunting routine.

◆ As you locate job postings and relevant contacts using the tools described in the next section, you'll need some way of keeping track of names, phone numbers, interview times and dates, company information, and so on. Consider creating a "job search" notebook for this purpose—a three-ring binder in which you can keep contact information, a calendar, and any relevant paperwork.

◆ Develop and maintain a support network of friends, family members, co-workers, and, if available, job counselors. Communicate with each member of your network on a regular basis.

◆ Stay positive, even if the search drags on longer than you'd like.

◆ Be good to yourself. Searching for a job can be difficult and stressful under the best of circumstances! Eat right, exercise, and get enough sleep, and make sure to allow yourself some down time.

What's Out There: Finding the Job for You

In the old days, finding a job meant scouring the help-wanted ads in the local Sunday paper and crossing one's fingers. These days, finding a job involves a multi-pronged, targeted assault on the following fronts:

◆ Your school's career center

◆ The Internet

◆ Your personal network of contacts

◆ Career fairs

◆ Help-wanted newspaper ads

YOUR SCHOOL'S CAREER CENTER

Whether you're still in school, a newly minted college graduate, or have been in the real world for a spell, make your school's career center your first stop in your job search. Here are some of the resources you can expect to find there:

◆ A database of current job listings

◆ Access to staff career counselors

◆ Career path information

◆ Counseling and resources for students interested in applying to graduate school

◆ A repository for letters of reference for employment or for admission to graduate school

◆ Resources to help you compile a winning résumé and write an exceptional cover letter

◆ Career fairs and access to corporate recruiters

◆ Career-planning workshops and programs

THE INTERNET

Beyond what's available at your school's career center, the Internet offers a vast resource for the job seeker. You'll find myriad sites geared to help you land employment.

General Job-Search Sites

The Internet is stuffed with general job-search sites—that is, sites that post jobs which aren't limited to a particular industry or field. In addition to boasting literally hundreds of thousands of job postings, the best of these sites offer useful career and job-search advice, tools for determining an appropriate salary range for the position you seek, the ability to e-mail you when jobs that match your criteria are posted, and resources to help you research companies that catch your eye. Here are just a few general job-search sites you'll want to explore:

◆ CareerBuilder (www.careerbuilder.com)

◆ DirectEmployers.com (www.directemployers.com)

◆ Monster.com (www.monster.com)

◆ Quint Careers (www.quintcareers.com)

◆ Vault (www.vault.com)

◆ WetFeet (www.wetfeet.com)

◆ Yahoo! HotJobs (www.hotjobs.com)

Industry-Specific Sites

In addition to browsing the various general job-search sites online, you'll want to consider checking out some Web-based industry-specific search services.

For jobs in **finance, banking, insurance,** or **accounting,** check out these sites:

◆ *BankingBoard.com (www.bankingboard.com).* If you're looking for work in the mortgage, banking, escrow, or real-estate industry, you may want to visit BankingBoard.com.

◆ *BankJobs.com (www.bankjobs.com).* Post your résumé and search for jobs in banks and other financial institutions here.

◆ *CareerBank.com (www.careerbank.com).* In addition to providing résumé-posting, job-search, and career-development resources for job candidates in the fields of accounting, finance, and banking, CareerBank.com offers up-to-date industry news, articles, and newsletters.

◆ *eFinancialCareers (www.efinancialcareers.com).* This UK-based site aims to serve the global financial community by helping fill jobs in the securities, investment-banking, and asset-management industries. No matter where you're looking to work—at home or abroad—this site can help.

◆ *Financial Jobs (www.financial-jobs.com).* Candidates for careers in banking, accounting, corporate finance, or investment banking may find their dream job at Financial Jobs.

◆ *GreatInsuranceJobs.com (www.greatinsurancejobs.com).* In addition to providing job listings, this site lists a toll-free phone number in case candidates want to speak with someone in person. You'll also find industry-specific career guidance and tips on topics ranging from interviewing to salary negotiations.

◆ *IFSjobs.com (www.ifsjobs.com).* Focused on the converging insurance and financial services industries, IFSjobs.com seeks to match talented candidates with employers.

◆ *Insurance Job Channel (www.insurancejobchannel.com).* This Web portal offers, in its own words, "unparalleled access to insurance jobs in the USA." In addition to listing available positions at insurance firms nationwide, Insurance Job Channel (IJC) lists the names and addresses of every major insurance company in the nation and provides direct links to each company's website.

◆ *Jobs in the Money (www.jobsinthemoney.com).* Touted by *Forbes* magazine as one of the best around, this site is designed to link job seekers with prospective employers in accounting, banking, insurance, and investment banking.

◆ *StreetJobs.com (www.streetjobs.com).* Unlike other online job sites, which the folks at StreetJobs.com describe as "catch-all electronic bulletin boards," StreetJobs.com is a search firm that employs experienced search executives to facilitate and manage contact between employers and candidates. StreetJobs.com exclusively serves candidates and employers in domestic and international banks (both commercial and investment), as well as brokerage firms.

Visit the following sites for jobs in **marketing, advertising,** or **sales:**

◆ *AdJobsInc.com (www.adjobsinc.com).* This site facilitates communication between advertising professionals and ad agencies, offering job seekers listings of available jobs, information about various companies, a résumé database, and other job-search tools.

◆ *MarketingJobs.com (www.marketingjobs.com).* Search for jobs in sales, marketing, advertising, and public relations at MarketingJobs. com. In the Career Center you can access the site's professional résumé service, a salary calculator, and a bookstore offering titles geared toward sales, marketing, advertising, and public relations professionals.

◆ *SalesJobs.com (www.salesjobs.com).* This site, mentioned by *Forbes* magazine in its list of top job sites, is geared toward matching sales professionals with the job of their dreams. As noted by *Forbes,* however, SalesJobs.com is "all about the jobs"; you won't find much in the way of educational content.

◆ *Talent Zoo (www.talentzoo.com).* This site, aimed at candidates interested in working in advertising, is yet another site that has been plugged by *Forbes.* In addition to finding job postings for account execs, art directors, media buyers, and their colleagues, Talent Zoo boasts scads of useful—not to mention pithy—articles for navigating those choppy advertising waters.

Job Sites for Students/Recent College Grads

A few job sites are geared toward college students and recent grads. In addition to matching prospective employers with college-educated candidates, these sites often contain extra material meant to help those transitioning from college life to the "real world." Here are a few you might want to check out:

◆ *AfterCollege (www.aftercollege.com).* AfterCollege works directly with faculty and student group officers to match students seeking jobs with employers—often of the Fortune 500 variety.

◆ *AlumniRecruiter.com (www.alumnirecruiter.com).* In addition to featuring a database of tens of thousands of great jobs, this site boasts a continuing education wizard designed to help you find the graduate school program that best suits your needs.

◆ *CampusCareerCenter.com (www.campuscareercenter.com).* This site aims to match the best and the brightest college grads with Fortune 500 companies nationwide. It also features scads of advice geared toward students and recent grads.

◆ *CollegeGrad.com (www.collegegrad.com).* CollegeGrad.com claims to provide more entry-level job search content than any other site. In addition to loads of job listings, you'll find résumé templates, salary information, and more.

◆ *MonsterTRAK (www.monstertrak.monster.com).* Backed by job-search behemoth Monster.com, MonsterTRAK offers employers direct access to job seekers through partnerships with college and university career centers. Utilized by more than 600,000 employers, MonsterTRAK is the most-visited college-targeted site on the Internet.

Company Websites

If a particular company has caught your eye, visit its website. Many companies post jobs on their sites, enabling you to get the most current information about job openings as well as apply directly with the click of a button. You may even be able to find information about career paths, corporate culture, benefits and compensation, and more. If the company that interests you isn't quite that technically savvy, odds are you'll at the very least find the name or e-mail address of the person in charge of hiring; use it to contact him or her directly.

Of course, actually *finding* the company's site may prove frustrating. Your best bet is to Google the company (that is, to enter the company's name in the Search field at www.google.com) and link to the company's site from there. Alternatively, visit the following Web pages, where you can link directly to the career and employment section of some 4,000 company websites:

◆ First Steps in the Hunt (www.interbiznet.com/hunt/companies)

◆ The Quintessential Directory of Company Career Centers (www.quintcareers.com/career_centers)

NETWORKING

You know the saying, "It's not *what* you know, it's *who* you know." Which is why it's imperative you plumb your contacts, a process referred to in civilized circles as "networking," to see if they can help you land the job of your dreams. Here are a few places to start:

◆ Fellow students, friends, and family

◆ Alumni organizations

◆ Professional organizations

Fellow Students, Friends, and Family

If Kevin Bacon is within six degrees of separation from every other actor in the history of film, then surely you're within six degrees of a person who can hire *you*. Consider all the people you know, even casually: family members, co-workers, professors, classmates, roommates, teammates, fraternity brothers or sorority sisters, neighbors, members of your congregation, people at your gym . . . the list is long! Then, figure that all those people have a list that's equally long, and all *those* people have a list that's equally long, and pretty soon you're looking at enough people to populate the Netherlands.

So how do you figure out who among your friends' friends' friends can help you? Start talking. Call around. Send some e-mails. You never know—your Pilates instructor might have an uncle in investment banking who'd be willing to help you out.

Just remember, if someone goes to bat for you, show some gratitude. Buy your instructor a soy Chai latte and send her uncle a thank-you card (or whatever seems appropriate). Along the same lines, be on the lookout for ways in which you can help others. If you stumble upon an opening that fits your buddy Mike to a "T," by all means pass it on. Then make Mike swear on his X-Box that he'll do the same for you.

Alumni Organizations

Fellow alumni from your college or university are great networking resources, so make it a point to get involved with your school's alumni association. For example, my alumni association offers members access to an online alumni directory and career help center, regional clubs, constituent societies (such as the Law Alumni), and more, and hosts events nationwide to help alumni connect. It may just turn out that the CEO of your dream company graduated from your alma mater, and loves to help fellow alums get a leg up in her industry!

Professional Organizations

Some college graduates know exactly what field they want to enter. If you're one such graduate, consider joining the professional organization that represents that field to expand your network. For example, if you know you want to work in the health care sector, consider joining the American College of Healthcare Executives. Doing so gives you access to the organization's 30,000 members.

Look, too, for organizations in your field that reflect your cultural heritage or gender. For example, the National Association of Black Telecommunications Professionals aims, in its own words, "to be the premier source of education and information regarding the telecommunications industry for our members, interfacing organizations, and the public, with a specific emphasis on the African-American community." Likewise, Business and Professional Women is the leading advocate for working women, regardless of their field.

To find an association that caters to your sector, visit one of the following websites:

◆ *Associations on the Net (www.ipl.org/div/aon)*. The Internet Public Library has compiled this directory of organizations with a Web presence. Simply click a category to drill down to your field of interest.

◆ *The ASAE Gateway to Associations Directory (www.asaenet.org/cda/ asae/associations_search/1,3200,MEN3,00.html?AlliedSocietyCode= ALL&submit=Go%21)*. Search for an association by name, interest area, geographic location, or some combination thereof.

CAREER FAIRS

Career fairs or job fairs are a great way to make face-to-face contact with recruiters from numerous companies. Generally, you'll find advertisements announcing career fairs in your local newspaper or through your school's career center.

To ensure that you make a lasting impression with recruiters at a career fair, consider the following tips:

◆ Find out beforehand what companies will be represented at the career fair, and decide which ones interest you most. That way, on the day of the fair, you can target only those companies that interest you, bypassing booths for companies in industries outside your area of expertise.

◆ Research the companies whose booths you plan to visit, and include a cheat sheet about each one in your briefcase. Then, before you approach a company's booth, review your cheat sheet to refresh your memory. Being armed with a few key facts about the company will go a long way toward impressing a recruiter.

◆ In order to make a good first impression, rehearse your approach in front of a mirror at home or with a friend. Hammer out a one-minute synopsis of your skills and experience, which you can recite after smiling, introducing yourself, and shaking each recruiter's hand (while looking him or her in the eye, of course). Practice speaking clearly and confidently while maintaining a friendly and conversational tone.

◆ Prepare a question or two for each recruiter in advance. For example, you might ask the recruiter what he or she likes about working for the company, or what the company's long-term goals are.

◆ Dress as you would for a job interview, carrying only a briefcase. (See the section "Dress" under "Acing the Interview" later in this chapter for more information.) In the event of inclement weather, check your winter coat or raincoat at the venue's coatroom (if available) so you don't have to haul it around.

◆ Be sure to bring several copies of your résumé with you—more than you think you'll need. As the folks at Yahoo! Hot Jobs note, "You don't want to find yourself halfway through the career fair and realize that you've run out."

HELP-WANTED ADS

Help-wanted ads are far from obsolete; indeed, as noted on About.com, many businesses rely on placing help-wanted ads in their local newspaper for all their hiring needs to limit the pool of candidates to a manageable number. Of course, one way to access help-wanted ads placed in your local paper is to buy the paper. Alternatively, see if your local paper (or the paper in the city to which you plan to relocate) publishes an online edition with searchable ads.

Landing a Position

Locating a job is one thing; *landing* it is another. This section steps you through the hiring process, from writing a killer résumé and cover letter to submitting your application materials to acing the interview.

WRITING A KILLER RÉSUMÉ

Because managers and HR professionals receive such vast numbers of résumés each day, they must, in the words of Vault.com, "look for any deficiency possible to reduce the applicant pool to a manageable number." That means it's up to you to generate a résumé that enables employers to assess your skills, qualifications, and experience quickly and easily.

Many books have been written about crafting a superior résumé; an extensive discussion of this topic is beyond the scope of this book. However, here are some points to keep in mind:

◆ Favor brief bullet points that concisely summarize your experiences and qualifications over long, dense paragraphs. Avoid using vague or flowery language. Embrace the use of action phrases ("Launched startup on-campus coffee cart") over cumbersome complete sentences ("I personally launched a company geared toward serving coffee and related beverages to my fellow students").

◆ "Right-size" your résumé. Making it too short highlights your inexperience; making it too long discourages recruiters from reading your résumé in its entirety. As suggested by the folks at Monster.com, "Focus on the skills and accomplishments that directly apply to the job you're trying to get. Every word counts, so don't dwell on the specifics of each job, but rather the highlights specific to you."

◆ With so many companies using computer technology to store résumés, it's imperative that you craft yours so that it is scannable. That means sprinkling relevant keywords throughout. In addition, according to Monster.com, you should ensure that letters in your chosen font do not touch (a sans-serif font such as Arial, with a font size of between 10 and 14 points, is a good choice); avoid using columns; employ round, solid (as opposed to hollow) bullets; shun the use of ampersands, percent signs, and so on; and steer clear of paper containing dark speckles.

◆ Customize your résumé for each prospective employer to highlight your qualifications and experiences that are most relevant to the position. Determine which skills each employer is seeking and craft your résumé accordingly.

◆ Use numbers to quantify your achievements. For example, instead of writing "Recruited students for study," try "Recruited 75 students to participate in 12-month study."

◆ Many job sites, such as Monster.com and CareerGrad.com, offer résumé templates. Plugging your information into such a template can help you pull together a winning résumé.

◆ If at first you don't succeed, and trying and trying again hasn't yielded much in the way of tangible results, consider hiring a professional résumé writer to help you nail yours down. You can find résumé pros at Monster.com and Vault.com.

◆ Be sure to proofread your résumé before sending it out. Correct all typos, grammatical errors, malapropisms, and other blunders. Your failure to do so may lead prospective employers to conclude that you are a) careless or b) not the brightest bulb on the tree. Neither conclusion bodes well for you.

WRITING AN OUTSTANDING COVER LETTER

As noted by Katharine Hansen and Randall S. Hansen, Ph.D., authors of *Dynamic Cover Letters* and frequent contributors to QuintCareers. com, "A résumé is useless to an employer if he or she doesn't know what kind of work you want to do. A cover letter tells the employer the type of position you're seeking—and exactly how you are qualified for that position." Cover letters can also be used to "highlight the aspects of your experience that are most useful to the potential employer" (the Hansens note that "you can earn points for knowing what those aspects are"), can "explain things that your résumé can't" (such as gaps in your employment history), and can help you convey your personality in a way your résumé cannot.

Unlike your résumé, which you may or may not tailor depending on the criteria listed by a particular ad or job posting, cover letters must be crafted with a specific employer and job in mind. As you craft each individual cover letter, keep these tips in mind:

◆ Send the cover letter to a specific individual in the company rather than "to whom it may concern" (or what have you). Otherwise, there's a strong possibility your résumé will be immediately discarded.

◆ Grab your reader's attention in the first paragraph—indeed, the first *sentence*—by explaining why you are writing the letter and briefly outlining how you can meet the company's needs. Make it interesting!

◆ If a member of your network turned you onto the company or job about which you are enquiring, drop his or her name prominently in the letter.

◆ Just as your résumé should favor brief bullet points that concisely summarize your experiences and qualifications over long, dense paragraphs, so too should your cover letter—although you should not use the cover letter to simply rehash your résumé.

◆ Unlike your résumé, which may be longer than one page should your experience merit that, a cover letter should never require a second sheet of paper. A cover letter containing four brief paragraphs should be adequate.

◆ Be specific. Don't just say you feel you'd be an asset to the company; say *why*, citing concrete evidence and using examples when possible.

◆ Be proactive by requesting an interview, and promise to follow up with a phone call. (Of course, you must then *make* said phone call.)

◆ In addition to offering résumé templates, many job sites such as Monster.com and CareerGrad.com offer cover letter templates to help you generate your missives. These can be helpful, but avoid relying on them too heavily; otherwise, your cover letter may end up reading exactly like those of countless other job seekers.

◆ If you need additional help, consider submitting your cover letter to a site such as Vault.com for a critique. It'll cost you, but it might be worth it.

◆ Sign your name legibly, boldly, and confidently.

◆ Be sure to proofread every cover letter before sending it out.

APPLYING FOR THE JOB

Many companies enable job candidates to apply for open positions online. This trend benefits the job seeker in myriad ways. For one, it eliminates the need for job seekers to purchase expensive résumé paper and stamps. Applying online can also make it easier to keep track of jobs to which you've applied, because most companies send a confirmation e-mail upon receipt of your electronically submitted application.

However you choose to apply to a job—online or via regular mail—be certain to follow the application instructions to the letter. For example, some company websites prohibit applicants from sending attachments with their online applications, instead asking you to paste your résumé and cover letter into the spaces provided. Other companies ask applicants to include the job code for the position for which they are applying. Whatever the instructions, your failure to follow them may prompt those reviewing applications to toss yours without even considering it.

ACING THE INTERVIEW

If your résumé and cover letter have enticed a company to contact you for an interview, you've cleared the first big hurdle. Now it's time to prepare for the big day.

Preparation

According to Monster.com, the 10 most common interview questions are:

◆ Tell me about yourself.

◆ Why did you leave or are you leaving your last position?

◆ What do you know about this company?

◆ What are your goals?

◆ What are your strengths and weaknesses?

◆ Why do you want to work for this company?

◆ What has been your most significant achievement?

◆ How would your last boss and colleagues describe you?

◆ Why should we hire you?

◆ What are your salary expectations?

Before your interview, you must carefully consider these questions and devise an honest, articulate answer to each one. In addition, prepare answers to a few behavioral questions (for example, "Tell me about a time when . . . " or "Give me an example of . . . " type questions).

You'll also want to prepare for your interview by doing the following:

◆ Research the company thoroughly before the interview. Scour the company's website for information, comb through recent issues of industry trade journals for mentions of the company, and Google the company to see if any recent news stories pop up. Talk with some current or former employees to get a sense of the company's culture and direction. The more you can demonstrate what you know about the company during your interview, the better impression you'll make.

◆ Prepare some insightful questions of your own to demonstrate that you've done your homework about the company.

◆ Practice your interviewing technique either in front of the mirror or by engaging in a mock interview with a professional at your school's career center or with a friend. Consider not only your answers to the mock interview questions, but also your facial expressions, eye contact, handshake, and body language.

◆ Prepare a fact sheet that lists your skills, qualifications, and accomplishments to help you stay focused during the interview.

◆ Before the interview, assemble in your briefcase several copies of your résumé, a copy of your references, a pad of paper, and a pen, along with directions to the interview site.

Dress

At some colleges (mine comes to mind), rolling out of bed and staggering to class wearing one's pajama bottoms, a sweatshirt, and a baseball cap is common practice, and is in no way detrimental to one's ability to succeed both academically and socially. Likewise, students sporting piercings, tattoos, and hair colors not found in nature are scarcely noticed. In the "real world," however, especially for those students seeking to enter the world of business, standards of dress and hygiene are somewhat more stringent and conservative.

Witness the 2001 survey conducted by the National Association of College and Employers (NACE), which asked employers to evaluate a list of 10 physical attributes and indicate how much each attribute neg-atively influenced the employer's opinion of a candidate's suitability. On a 3-point scale, grooming garnered a 2.6 rating, with nontradi-tional interview attire earning a 2.3. Chiming in with ratings of 2.0 were nontraditional hair color, obvious tattoos, and body piercings.

The bottom line? In the words of NACE executive director Marilyn Mackes, "A candidate's overall appearance is likely to give a potential employer pause." That means if your goal is to find gainful employ-ment in business, you'll need to dress accordingly. You can't go wrong if you dress like an executive, which generally means the following:

◆ Wear a conservative two-piece business suit (solid dark blue or gray is best), paired with a simple white or pastel long-sleeved shirt. Men should wear a silk necktie with a traditional print.

◆ Make sure the clothes you're wearing are clean and well-pressed.

◆ Your shoes should be conservative, clean, and polished. For men, black lace-ups are best; women should wear shoes with a moder-ate heel.

◆ Hosiery should be subtle—that means dark socks (black is best) for men, and skin-color, run-free pantyhose for women.

◆ Hair should be well-groomed and simply arranged. For men, short hair is best, sans mustache or beard.

◆ Hands should be scrupulously clean with fingernails neatly trimmed. Women should wear a muted shade of nail polish, if any.

◆ Keep jewelry to a minimum. Men should wear at most a wedding ring or college ring, and no earrings. Women should wear no more than one ring on each hand, and only one set of earrings—simple studs are best. It goes without saying that nose rings, eyebrow rings, and the like are right out.

◆ Minimal—if any—cologne or perfume should be worn. Along these lines, women should wear minimal makeup; it should not be too noticeable.

◆ Carry a light briefcase or portfolio case and nothing else—not even a purse. Empty your pockets of any phones, coins, or what have you, placing items in the case.

Manners

If you've managed to land an interview, the company already knows you have the skills it's looking for. The interview, then, is all about personality. Are you pleasant to be around? Can you get along with others? Being on your best behavior, a.k.a. "minding your manners," during the interview can go a long way toward landing you the job. Keep these points in mind:

◆ Be punctual. There's no excuse for lateness, period. Indeed, savvy applicants arrive a few minutes early to allow time to find the interview location, hit the loo (be sure to take one last look at yourself in the mirror to make sure you don't have any spinach in your teeth, and spit out your gum while you're there), and review their notes (though, presumably, not in the loo).

◆ Be polite to everyone you meet while at the interview location, from the janitor to the receptionist to the interviewer to prospective co-workers.

◆ Offer a firm—but not crushing—handshake when introduced to your interviewer. Maintain eye contact and *smile.*

◆ Mark Twain once said "'Be yourself' is the worst advice you can give some people," but we're pretty sure he was kidding. During your interview, you should be, well, *you*—but on your best, most professional behavior. (Be warned: Some recruiters may pretend to be your new best friend in an attempt to lull you into revealing an aspect of your personality best kept under wraps. If this happens to you, be friendly, but remain professional and attempt to steer the discussion back to your strengths.)

◆ Relax. Treat the interview as you would a conversation with someone you respect.

◆ Be flexible. If someone can't meet with you at precisely the time you agreed on, deal with it gracefully.

◆ Be positive, direct, clear, and concise in your answers, and above all, be truthful. Provide concrete examples to bolster your answer. If asked a difficult question, such as "Why were you fired from your last job?" attempt to convey your answer in as positive a manner as possible—for example, focusing on what the experience taught you instead of railing against your evil ex-boss.

◆ Show interest in the company and in the interviewer. Ask questions that demonstrate what you learned about the company during the course of your research before the interview.

◆ Don't rush. Experts suggest you allow at least two hours for the interview, so plan accordingly.

◆ Under no circumstances should you bring up the subject of salary, vacation, or benefits during the interview. These topics are best discussed *after* an offer has been made. If, during the course of the interview, you are asked to provide your salary expectations, answer truthfully, but note that salary is negotiable.

◆ When the interview is over, thank the interviewer. To make a more lasting impression, send a hand-written thank-you note within 24 hours of the interview. Doing so demonstrates your interest in the position and can even help break a tie between you and another candidate who skips this crucial step. Be sure the note contains no spelling or grammatical errors, and is written neatly!

## Chapter 7

Case Studies

This chapter contains five case studies showcasing people who majored in business as an undergraduate or obtained an MBA. These case studies are designed to convey what types of jobs are available to the business student, why each case study subject chose to pursue a degree in business, and how his or her business studies have proved beneficial at work. You'll also read about smart moves each subject made during the course of his or her career, as well as pitfalls to avoid. All of this is meant to help you determine whether a business degree is the right choice for you.

Matt: Product Director

Matt, who majored in business at the University of Colorado, works at a sporting-goods company as the Director of Baseball and Softball Products. Classmate connections were crucial for Matt in landing his first job at the company—in the finance department—right out of college. Matt's job offers many perks, including annual business trips to such sporting events as the NCAA Baseball College World Series, the MLB All-Star Game, and the World Series.

WHAT I DO

I am the Director of Baseball and Softball Products at a major sporting-goods manufacturer. I am responsible for all the baseball and softball product lines at the company, including the following:

◆ Setting the business plan for the division

◆ Working with sales to develop our yearly sales budgets

◆ Identifying and developing new products

◆ Managing the product managers who look after 13 product lines

◆ Providing a worldwide forecast for all baseball/softball products on a quarterly basis

◆ Working with our factories and sourced vendors to ensure quality products are made on time

◆ Working with promotions to get professional and collegiate players the products they need

◆ Presenting the product lines to our international sales force as well as to our largest retail accounts

WHY I CHOSE TO PURSUE A BUSINESS DEGREE

I decided to major in business during my senior year in high school. I liked the idea of working in international business. I wanted to travel and was always interested in how companies are run. I liked how different companies have images and ways of doing businesses and the strategies of what works for each company.

HOW MY BUSINESS DEGREE PREPARED ME FOR MY JOB

Classmate connections worked for me. I got my first job at the company through a friend of mine who went to the business school at Colorado with me. The finance and marketing classes I took in college definitely helped give me the proper perspective, as well as some of the direct skills that I needed to adapt and excel at my job in the Finance department (my first job at the company). I believe it gave me a running start to my business career.

ADDITIONAL TRAINING

I received a B.S. in business with a double emphasis in finance and marketing. I have not taken any other course work and do not have an MBA. I have done most of my business training on the job as I have worked my way up through the company. I worked in the finance/ accounting department for one year, and then worked as a product sourcing manager for three years, where I was responsible for product development communications with our sourced vendors. I was then the bat product manager for two years, in charge of the bat line. For the last seven years I have held my current position. Moving around within the company from the finance department to the operations department and finally to marketing gave me a great education as to how the whole of the company works. I consider this my best education.

Helpful Moves

My business degree got me looking for the right types of jobs. The rest was just luck that I got a job in the sporting-goods industry (through the contact my friend gave me). Because I was a huge sports fan and extremely interested in the industry as a career, I made the decision to take any job offered to me so that I could get my foot in the door. My first job in accounting was not my first choice of departments, but I felt it was important to take any job within the company just to get in. I felt that I could work my way into a more attractive position once I got acclimated to the company and was able to look around for areas that I felt were exciting.

Pitfalls to Avoid

Don't set your sights on the ultimate job right out of college and reject anything less. If you are passionate about a certain industry or company, I would strongly recommend doing all you can to get in, even if it is not in the job that you are ultimately interested in. It is very difficult to get a product manager job right out of college in the relatively small sporting-goods industry. Most of our hires have come from within the company, where someone has taken a job in operations or customer service. Be confident that you will be able to network within the company or industry to get the more desirable positions.

What I Love about My Job

I love my job. The baseball industry is very exciting to me. I love working for a company that is dedicated to making the highest-quality products in our industry. I love the challenges that constantly come up. I love working for a company that is growing so rapidly. We have doubled in size over the past four years and continue to grow at double-digit rates. I like interacting with the retail side of things—our large customers. I also enjoy working with athletes to give them the equipment they need to perform well. I like setting strategies and working as a team to execute them successfully. Most of all, I like to compete and enjoy being with a company that performs well.

THINGS ON THE JOB I COULD DO WITHOUT

I do not like watching organizational problems go unaddressed. Whether it's an individual who is taking advantage of his or her position or an ineffective structure, I think it is demoralizing to see these types of problems persist. I think most good employees feel that they work hard and want to be rewarded for it. They also feel taken advantage of if the playing field is not equal and other functional areas are not putting in the time or effort that they are, yet are allowed to remain that way.

MY WORK AND MY LIFE

I work from about 7:30 to 5:30. I travel a lot (at least a week every month). The pay is very good as I have a bonus tied to company and division performance. Both the company and division have done very well over the past seven years. I get three weeks of vacation and usually don't use it all. I get to go on many business trips every year that keep things fun—the NCAA Baseball College World Series, the MLB All-Star Game, the World Series, a few trade shows, and so on. I am married with two daughters (ages 5 and 3). The travel is a little heavy, but I spend a lot of time with them when I am at home. I make my family my priority when I am not at work. I work out and run about four days a week at the gym in our office and play golf whenever possible. Almost everyone thinks that I have an awesome job. Most of that is due to the fact that I interact with professional baseball players, which sounds very glamorous. I also work in an industry that is associated with fun and with being young.

Petra: Project Leadership Consultant

Armed with a business degree from her undergraduate studies as well as an MBA, Petra is a partner in a small leadership consulting group that focuses on medical device product development and launch. Project leadership, unlike project management, focuses on leading people rather than managing tasks. Petra enjoys a flexible schedule on a broad basis and good pay, and describes her work as "interesting and challenging."

WHAT I DO

I am a partner in a small (fewer than $5 million) project leadership consulting group. We have four partners and between 10 and 15 contract project leaders. We provide project leadership skills by leading or co-leading projects, coaching, mentoring, training, and providing "loan" or "temporary" executive services to a broad group of industries and functional areas. We market our services almost exclusively through word of mouth; we have a high level of returning clients and referrals.

Although the largest segment of our practice is in medical device product development and launch, I focus on business change strategy; rationalization (product, customer, and manufacturing); and corporate and data-center relocation or reconfiguration.

Our business strategy is, "Do the work we enjoy doing in a quality manner, always provide value to the customer, create a good environment for our people to work in, and give back to the community." To the last item, we have funded a nonprofit segment of our business to focus on the issues associated with the ineffectiveness and inefficiencies voiced by the foundations as they try to execute strategy.

Within the partnership, I focus my efforts on financial planning (we are reasonably profitable but need to manage cash flow in a growing business), strategic direction versus opportunistic projects, and being a team player.

WHY I CHOSE TO PURSUE A BUSINESS DEGREE

I based my decision to major in business on the following factors:

◆ Foundation skills in business are required to be successful in almost all disciplines.

◆ Business is about people and communicating with them. It's about vision, objectives, strategy, plans execution, adjustments, and completion.

◆ Majoring in business would provide me the ability to do many different things and experience many different people and places.

◆ Majoring in business would provide a career that I would enjoy and would provide the time and resources to enjoy the rest of my interests (family, hobbies, and lifelong learning).

I focused on accounting (BS) and finance (MBA), because even if you never practice those skills, your decision making is often based on them or a large consideration. Too many business people fail because they don't understand the financial implications of their decisions or strategies.

Of course, I wasn't able to articulate these decision criteria quite so clearly when I was 18 years old. Nor did I exactly understand all this at the time. What I realized was that although all decisions closed some doors, a decision to get a business degree only closed a few doors. As I entered business school, I gravitated to accounting because I had already held several jobs in businesses that weren't doing well because people couldn't understand basic finance.

How My Business Degree Prepared Me for My Job

My business major prepared me for my job in the following ways:

◆ It provided me with analytical discipline and skills.

◆ It taught me that there is always more than one right answer (however, it took me 20 years to remember this one).

◆ It taught me to maintain a big-picture, multidiscipline perspective—not just marketing, not just sales, and so on.

◆ I learned important business terms and models.

◆ I gained important real-world experiences (internships) that gave me a sense of reality that sometimes gets lost in a classroom.

◆ I learned that smart people are still just *people*.

ADDITIONAL TRAINING

I didn't *have* to obtain a graduate degree. But after I came out of undergraduate school, I worked for a small company and realized I really didn't have the breadth of understanding I needed to succeed in a small business. I went back after two years and got an MBA in finance to better understand the larger picture.

Early career experiences (namely, with Arthur Andersen Consulting) provided me with the opportunity to work all over the world, in all different industries, with all different issues and business problems. I immediately learned that I would never know it all (tough day), and that it was far more important to have the skill to recognize what you *don't* know. (This is very, *very* important.) Next, develop the skill to learn how to find the people who know what you don't. Work with them and provide them with the ability to help you and enjoy doing it.

The truth is, I learn something on every job I take. Sometimes it's "Well, I'll never do *that* again!" Most often, I learn from my mistakes. I find it very difficult to learn from successes. Successes build confidence. Mistakes help you learn to do it right.

HELPFUL MOVES

Here are a few things I've learned along the way that may be helpful:

◆ Manage your résumé. Always keep it up to date.

◆ Job security is between the ears.

◆ Always grow your network. You never know where the next opportunity will come from.

◆ In most jobs, success is best measured by whether management wants you to work on the next big opportunity, and whether your peers and team members want to work with you.

◆ Success is not measured in dollars.

◆ Never stop learning and never stop growing.

◆ Use the skills you learned in school not to manage your career as the end goal, but to find balance in your life between career, family, and other interests.

PITFALLS TO AVOID

Here's some advice to help you avoid some pitfalls:

◆ Take the long view. Every job and every assignment has its bad parts.

◆ Don't bitch about things. Either change them, endure them, or leave. Bitching is just a waste of time and energy.

◆ Don't worry about missing an opportunity. There is an unlimited number of opportunities. The only potential limiting factor is your creativity.

◆ If you don't understand why management did something, don't start by saying they are wrong. Instead, start by saying "I don't understand why they did that." Then think of three plausible reasons why they might have done what they did. This is a wonderful mental exercise to help you discipline your mind to think objectively in times of emotional stress.

◆ Don't ever stop learning, and don't start thinking that you know enough. Once you stop learning, you are just putting in the hours and hoping to hold on until you retire. Not a healthy environment.

◆ Work is not about the money and it's not about the power; it's about the ability to create your own space, share it with the ones you love, and give back to those less fortunate.

◆ Work is not about sacrificing your health, your life, or your family. A career should enhance your life goals, not define them.

◆ Don't waste time wishing other people would change. They won't.

◆ The more academic training we receive, especially business school, the more we incorrectly believe we can influence random events. If you're faced with a problem, don't worry about it; either do something about it or let go of it.

◆ Don't focus too much on the thing rather than the people. It always comes down to people.

◆ Don't believe you have to have the answer. All you need is to ask the right question to the right person.

WHAT I LOVE ABOUT MY JOB

I love several aspects of my job:

◆ New challenges

◆ Collaboration

◆ Starting and stopping

◆ New business being generated by meeting interesting people and connecting

◆ Giving back to the community

◆ Relative freedom to manage my schedule

◆ Meeting and working with great people

◆ Always learning new things

◆ Providing value

THINGS ON THE JOB I COULD DO WITHOUT

Here are a few things I could do without:

◆ First, second, and third, realize that every form of refuge has its price. If you don't like the price, try to change it or get a new refuge. Remember, the definition of insanity is you keep doing the same thing over and over and expecting a different outcome.

◆ Listening to people whine.

◆ Dealing with dysfunctional people.

◆ Handling 12-to-18-month projects.

MY WORK AND MY LIFE

My work day varies significantly, from

◆ Work at home office

◆ Work at client's all day

◆ Work at client's all day and at home all evening

◆ Work out in the morning, meet clients on boat in afternoon

◆ Work 30 hours in a row over the weekend doing disaster recovery

I have reasonably good control over my schedule on a broad basis. Pay is good; I put a very large amount into my 401(k). My schedule provides flex for family most of the time. The work is interesting and challenging. If I don't like a project, I know I'll have a new one soon.

Working with intelligent, bright, positive people is very motivating. I love to meet new talented people, work with them to achieve a goal, have them pay me, and most importantly, hear them say "thank you!"

Many people don't understand what I do. They either don't know what project leadership is or confuse it with project management. Project leaders lead people, and project managers manage tasks. Our skill set is like our logo: a balance between intuition and logic.

Gordon: Derivatives Strategist

After majoring in philosophy as an undergraduate, Gordon found his career mobility in the finance sector, his chosen field, somewhat limited. After obtaining an MBA and completing the Chartered Financial Analyst (CFA) program, Gordon landed a job as a derivatives strategist in a money-management firm, where he is charged with developing predictive insights on markets. Gordon enjoys the autonomy provided by his job, as well as reasonable hours and very high pay.

WHAT I DO

I work at a money-management firm as a derivatives strategist. My daily activities can be broken into two primary areas:

- ◆ Working with portfolio managers to identify situations where derivatives can and should be used in their portfolios

- ◆ Managing "overlay" portfolios of derivatives (futures and options) at my own discretion to generate incremental returns for our clients

WHY I CHOSE TO PURSUE AN MBA

My current job is considered part of the "buy-side" of the investment business—people who make the buy and sell decisions. Prior to going to business school, I worked on the "sell-side" of the business, where your role is to make recommendations to your clients and act as a broker. After having worked in that position for five years, I felt that I wasn't being challenged intellectually and liked the idea of being the decision-maker rather than someone merely providing recommendations, and I liked the idea of being the client. At that time, everyone I spoke to said that the road to the buy-side went through business school. I initially made several attempts to circumvent the B-school detour, but found that the jobs I could pursue were not significantly better than what I was already doing. Ultimately, I relented and applied to schools.

HOW MY MBA PREPARED ME FOR MY JOB

For my undergraduate degree, I attended a liberal arts college that didn't offer a business major. As a result, prior to attending business school the vast majority of my business, finance, and economics knowledge was learned on the job. The MBA provided a formal education in these key areas and a solid foundation to put to work when faced with new situations. Even though the terminology used in the workplace may be different than what was learned in the classroom, it all comes down to the same constructs and if you know those, you are much better off. My job also involves a lot of statistical work. Many of the quantitative techniques that I use daily are based on things that I learned during the MBA program.

People talk about the "networking" that's gained from an MBA and I would tend to agree, though I'm not the heaviest user of the network. That said, I do know of numerous examples of people who have used the network of MBA grads to learn about job opportunities within their industry, learn about job opportunities in different industries, or just gain perspective on a company or business that they need to evaluate.

ADDITIONAL TRAINING

I completed the Chartered Financial Analyst (CFA) program a couple of years ago. You earn the right to use the designation CFA by passing a series of three annual tests administered by a private organization in Virginia, CFA Institute. The material they test covers a variety of financial instruments and research methods, the actual practice of portfolio management, and includes a heavy focus on ethical behavior. Though the studying was pretty time consuming, the program offers a great deal of practical knowledge and serves as a valuable signal to clients of your commitment to the industry and to protecting their interests.

HELPFUL MOVES

A vitally important decision that I made along the way was to use business school as an opportunity to truly challenge myself. A lot of people look at it as a two-year vacation, but I feel that my choice of a challenging curriculum (including several Ph.D.-level courses) and my decision to get something out of those courses has served me well in my current job.

PITFALLS TO AVOID

One potential pitfall for many is the tendency to romanticize a particular job or industry without much thought as to whether it is well suited to your interests and long-term goals. I did that somewhat coming out of undergrad with the Investment Banking industry. I thought it seemed so exciting and glamorous, but it was really just a high paycheck to offset a horrific lifestyle and generally boring entry-level work.

WHAT I LOVE ABOUT MY JOB

In general, I love the challenge of trying to come up with novel insights on markets that many people spend a great deal of time and energy trying to predict. The people are also generally a positive. Most are highly motivated and intelligent. The fact that results are by no means subjective is also a huge plus; the scoreboard is pretty easy to read at the end of the year, which somewhat decreases the political stuff that tends to go on in large organizations. My job also offers me a great deal of autonomy in setting my own schedule and agenda.

THINGS ON THE JOB I COULD DO WITHOUT

Some of the very things that I enjoy about the job are at times the sources of my greatest dislike for the job. At least once a month I question whether this is all worth it. Were some of my finance professors right in saying that the markets are efficient? Can you really maintain a consistent edge trying to win in a game that is followed by so many?

Also, having everything so objective can be pretty stressful. There's no sugar-coating bad performance. Unlike some other careers where you can often go on for some period of time unaware of your standing, in this job you have a feel for how you are doing on practically a daily basis. This can add some emotional volatility, as nothing ever moves in a straight line.

Finally, one of the realities of working in financial services is that the people running the company are very focused on profitability and operating efficiency. As a result, anyone who says that he or she has job security is living a myth and is probably most at risk of being fired.

MY WORK AND MY LIFE

I think the hours in this job are pretty reasonable relative to the pay. I like to come into the office early (around 6:45 A.M.), so I can get some work done before other things come up. This typically involves running reports and analyzing the results to come up with trade ideas for my portfolios. As the day gets going, I typically attend one or two 30- to 60-minute meetings with different fund teams. I also tend to initiate new trades in the morning.

Lunch is typically nonbusiness, talking sports or politics with friends in other parts of the company. The afternoons are often spent doing more analysis for other portfolios and calling or visiting portfolio managers to recommend strategies. Some other portion of the afternoon is typically spent monitoring performance of everything that is in place and reading research generated by other firms.

I typically head home between 5:30 and 6:00 P.M. That gets me home in time to see the kids and help put them to bed. I very rarely have to come into the office on weekends, but I typically spend some time each weekend doing some work-related reading.

As mentioned, pay is good—a healthy base salary that is enough to live on without my wife working, and a year-end bonus that can be anywhere from 50 to 150 percent of base. The bonus is good for putting away money for college for the kids, but it is highly variable. Benefits are good. Along with health care and dental, I get a parking space and four weeks of vacation (though I've never used more than three). I/we don't spend much money on hobbies and vacations. I go to a low-end gym most days before work and the kids take music and "My Gym" classes, but we tend to take most vacations to places where we can get free accommodations (i.e., Grandma's house).

Karl: Commercial Real Estate Attorney

Karl admits his career arc is the result of a "Taoist" approach, noting that he majored in business primarily as a way of avoiding fulfilling a foreign-language requirement, and opted for law school after an internship revealed he was not well suited to a career in business. In his current capacity, Karl structures commercial real-estate transactions and negotiates the terms of these transactions. Karl offers sage advice on juggling work and home life.

WHAT I DO

My primary job activities are as follows:

◆ Conferring with clients in person and via phone and e-mail

◆ Reviewing and drafting documents

◆ Communicating with opposing counsel

◆ Overseeing the legal aspects of real-estate transactions

◆ Directing/supervising attorneys with whom I work

The job responsibilities, though, are more interesting:

◆ Structuring the real-estate transactions (this means figuring out how the parts all fit together over the life of the project—the acquisition, development, leasing, equity investment, mortgage financing, and, finally, disposition)

◆ Negotiating the terms of the transaction at each of these steps

◆ Maximizing the upside/minimizing the downside for my client (this means structuring the transaction and negotiating the terms so that the client is protected as much as possible from downside risks such as environmental liability, while preserving for the client as much of the upside as possible, such as my client's "cut" after the mortgage lender and the equity investor are paid)

Oddly enough, as a lawyer, I charge based on the time spent performing job activities, but my value (and the reason anyone hires me at a high hourly rate) is my ability to handle the job responsibilities efficiently, effectively, and creatively. Go figure.

WHY I CHOSE TO PURSUE A BUSINESS MAJOR

My degree is from Indiana University-Bloomington. When I attended there, IU had a thing called the "University Division" for students who had not yet declared a major. It was intended that everyone would leave the University Division by the end of his or her sophomore year, but I left when they kicked me out as a senior. Having not yet declared a major, I wasn't in any of the "Colleges" or "Schools" and, consequently, neither I nor my records had a home. The University Division randomly sent my records to the College of Arts and Sciences English Department, which promptly rejected me (and my records) because I had not declared English as my major, nor had I been admitted to the College of A&S. Being a man in bureaucratic limbo, I decided that I'd better find a home at the School of Business. Already, I'd been taking business courses and was considering a business degree. Why? Because I had no aptitude for foreign languages, and the only IU degrees that could be obtained without taking a foreign language were from the School of Business or from the School of Health, Physical Education, and Recreation. I wasn't a jock (though I played a mean game of Ping-Pong at the time), so I opted for the School of Business. Some might view this as a decision by avoidance, but I prefer to see it as "going with the flow"—a kind of Taoist approach.

How My Business Major Prepared Me for My Job

My business major acquainted me with basic business concepts that I use on a day-to-day basis. Most importantly, though, IU offered an internship program that offered me the opportunity to work in the field for which I was being trained, and that led directly to determinations that (a) I was not well suited to a career in that field, and (b) I needed to find a better alternative (which, in my case, turned out to be law school).

Additional Training

Having determined that a better alternative was law school, I lined myself up for three years of graduate school and a JD (the cheap doctorate—skip the master's degree and go directly to juris doctor after only three short years). Then, the internships (or, in the parlance of lawyers, the "clerkships") were crucial. Clerkships lead directly to jobs, and everyone needed a job, so everyone needed a clerkship. My clerkship was a summer spent at Baker & Daniels getting paid two or three times what I was worth and being courted for a permanent position at the end of law school (well, more precisely, a permanent position at the end of law school and after passing the Bar exam, both of which are required for state licensure). I can't say that my undergraduate course work was particularly helpful, except that my business law class, at least, was interesting and introduced me to basic precepts of American law. Earlier jobs were helpful in ruling out certain other possible career choices, such as Grill Man at Wendy's.

Helpful Moves

Having adopted a Taoist/avoidance "strategy" as a student, I probably don't have much helpful advice on this front. In truth, while in college, I simply was too young and naive to understand that there were "strategies" to be adopted. In my view, life was something that, for the most part, just *happened* to you. My ability to adopt strategies for advancing myself and my career developed after both business and law school.

To discover strategies for advancing yourself in a large law firm, see the collected works of Machiavelli. Okay, I admit, that's slightly cynical. Work hard. Be creative. Maintain your integrity. Recognize and take opportunities when they present themselves. Here's one more helpful hint: When the dean of your school suggests that you apply for a scholarship or fellowship, it's probably a good idea to apply. My batting average in obtaining scholarship/fellowships suggested by the dean: 1,000.

PITFALLS TO AVOID

Don't take a billiards class for easy credit. I graduated from IU with a GPA of 3.997. It would have been a 4.0, but I got an A- in billiards. So, don't take billiards. Take bowling instead. I got an A in bowling. Better for the ol' GPA.

WHAT I LOVE ABOUT MY JOB

For the most part, I genuinely like the people I work with (but then, really, I'm not very choosy). I don't work "for" anyone but myself, which is one of the most satisfying aspects of my job. I'm not well suited to answering to external authority. That makes being your own boss a very good thing—the only authority to whom you must answer is yourself. Okay, it's not quite that pure. I have clients, partners, and employees to and for whom I am responsible and, therefore, answerable, but you get the point. Plus, the setting and the pay are good. Otherwise, my job is largely satisfying for the following reason: I'm responsible for solving problems creatively and implementing unique solutions. This means that, in large part, my job remains "fresh" and intellectually challenging.

THINGS ON THE JOB I COULD DO WITHOUT

There's always something about a job that we'd rather not do: paperwork, bureaucracy, and pointless meetings. Add to the list the frequent small-mindedness and short-sightedness of other people.

MY WORK AND MY LIFE

Let's cover money first. In that regard, suffice it to say I'm one of the people whose taxes John Kerry was so anxious to raise. That means I have money for hobbies and recreation. So, pay is excellent, benefits are good, and vacation time would be good if I were organized enough to organize more time off. That's my fault. My partners take plenty of vacations.

It used to be that I had little to no time for hobbies and recreation, and juggling work and personal life simply meant that work came first. That was back when I was an associate and partner at a large law firm and billed 2,100 hours per year. Now that I have my own firm, I bill around 1,600 hours per year. Figuring 40 hours per week means that I now have 12.5 more weeks of free time per year, which I would like to report that I spend going to the gym and pursuing fruitful activities that will improve society, but, in truth, I'm kind of lazy. So, although I go to the gym more (racquetball routinely three times per week, instead of once or twice), I really spend my free time reading novels and *The New Yorker,* seeing movies with my teenage sons, and generally hanging out at home.

Life would be pretty good if I hadn't ruined my marriage during the "big firm" hard-work years. But I did (well, actually, my wife helped ruin it, too; I didn't do it all by myself). Juggling work and personal life so that work comes first pretty much means you're likely to be juggling divorce as part of your later personal life. However, I now have as much time to spend with my sons as my sons can stand, teenagers having a natural limited tolerance for the company of their fathers.

In fact, I would have even more time at home if I were more efficient at work. To be more efficient, though, I would have to spend less time on personal calls and e-mails, shopping online, and hanging out in other people's offices. But this is a tradeoff I'm not likely to make. On the other hand, a fair amount of my time at work is spent on personnel issues (the soap-opera aspects of having your own business). I'd like to trade some of the soap-opera time. I'm still raising two boys. I'd like to not be "raising" anyone at work (my partners included).

Jeremy: Entrepreneur

Jeremy majored in business with a concentration in marketing at NYU and earned a minor in the fine arts. Subsequently, Jeremy obtained an MBA, also from NYU. This combination has served him well in his capacity as the owner of a small graphic-design studio. Because he is self-employed, Jeremy enjoys a flexible schedule, and enjoys his work—especially the artistic aspects—tremendously.

WHAT I DO

I run a small graphic design studio. I am responsible for pretty much everything: marketing, accounting, new business, keeping up with new technologies, etc., as well as designing materials for clients (websites, catalogs, brochures, and such).

WHY I MAJORED IN BUSINESS

I went to NYU's undergrad business school. At the time I thought it would give me some basic foundation for business and I figured that the education could be applied to whatever career I ended up in. I also minored in fine arts. I've always enjoyed drawing and art in general, so I thought about combining the two.

HOW MY BUSINESS MAJOR PREPARED ME FOR MY JOB

The degree (marketing) has helped me a little bit in running my own business. Honestly, I am not sure an undergraduate degree in business has been terribly helpful to me. Taking some courses in business is useful because it can help determine if you are interested in pursuing it further. Most of my business education that helps me now I learned from my graduate degree in business (MBA) as well as from work experience. I have found that my minor in fine arts has obviously helped me as well.

ADDITIONAL TRAINING

I also have an MBA from NYU (marketing, international business). When I finished undergrad, I worked for a year in a graphic design studio and applied to business school because I wasn't sure what I wanted to do and I thought that a business degree would give me something to either fall back on or use, depending on what I ended up doing.

HELPFUL MOVES

Minoring in fine arts was helpful because I received exposure to both the practical (studio courses) and historical aspects of art. Some of the marketing courses (in both undergrad and grad school) were helpful because I find myself using some of the strategies in determining clients' needs as well as promoting my own work.

PITFALLS TO AVOID

I am still not sure an undergraduate degree in business was the way to go for me. I think taking a broad selection of courses to gain exposure to a variety of subjects might be a better approach. Taking art courses definitely interested me more than the undergrad business courses, and sometimes I do feel that the journey to where I am now might have been a little smoother had I focused more on this area in undergrad.

WHAT I LOVE ABOUT MY JOB

I definitely enjoy creating and designing. I also enjoy helping a client determine the best approach or strategy to take when working on a piece for the client. Meeting with clients in different fields is also fun because I get to see how other industries work.

THINGS ON THE JOB I COULD DO WITHOUT

The accounting and drumming up new business can sometimes be annoying. Also, dealing with clients who have unrealistic expectations can be difficult—they have no budget, but they want to have the most incredible-looking brochure/website/ad, and they want it done in an hour.

MY WORK AND MY LIFE

My day depends on what the work load is. I try to get to the office by 9 A.M. (after dropping the kids off at school) and from there I check e-mail, return phone calls, and review my schedule to see what deadlines I have. Since I am basically self-employed, the hours are based on what work I have. I try not to stay too late, but if there is something pressing, I may not get home until late. I also try to get to the gym a few times a week during lunch or at the end of the day. People usually respond with an "oh, wow" when they hear I am a graphic designer, and if it even comes up, they are surprised to hear that I have a business degree.

Resources for the Business Major

This appendix includes loads of resources for the business major, from links to honor societies to books to handy websites.

Honor Societies for Business Majors

In addition to the numerous societies designed to honor students of all majors, such as Alpha Chi (www.alphachihonor.org), Lambda Sigma (www.lambdasigma.org), Mortar Board (www.mortarboard.org), Omicron Delta Kappa (www.odk.org), Phi Kappa Phi (www.phikappa phi.org), Golden Key (www.goldenkey.org), and the National Society of Collegiate Scholars (www.nscs.org), there are several societies geared specifically toward students majoring in business. Among other perks, these societies offer members access to an extensive alumni network. Honor societies for business students include the following:

◆ *Beta Gamma Sigma (www.betagammasigma.org).* This honor society serves business programs accredited by the Association to Advance Collegiate Schools of Business (AACSB) International. To join Beta Gamma Sigma, you must be in the highest 7 percent of your class as a junior, or in the upper 10 percent as a senior.

◆ *Delta Mu Delta (www.deltamudelta.org).* Delta Mu Delta is a national honor society for students of business administration.

Eligible students must have completed at least half the work required for their degree, have a cumulative GPA of .25 above a "B" or better, be in the top 20 percent of their class, and be in good standing.

◆ *Sigma Beta Delta (www.sigmabetadelta.org).* This society honors students who excel in their studies of business, management, and administration; eligible students rank in the upper 20 percent of their class.

◆ *Mu Kappa Tau (www.pse.org/mkt.asp).* Mu Kappa Tau, the Marketing Honor Society, offers international recognition for its members. Membership provides access to more than 11,000 members from more than 90 colleges nationwide. Membership is limited to marketing students who rank in the top 10 percent of their class as juniors or the top 20 percent of their class as seniors.

◆ *Omega Rho (http://omegarho.informs.org).* If your area of study encompasses operations research or management science, if you rank in the top 25 percent of your class, and if you have a GPA of 3.5 or higher (on a 4.0 scale), you are eligible for membership.

If you are eligible to join one of these societies but your school does not support a chapter, consider spearheading a movement to create one. This not only enables you to enjoy the privileges of membership, but also to cite your involvement in the creation of the chapter on your membership—something that's sure to demonstrate your leadership abilities!

Professional Societies for Business Majors

While you're in school, you have access to various co-ed fraternities designed to serve business students. These include the following:

◆ *Delta Sigma Pi (www.dspnet.org).* This co-ed professional business fraternity boasts more than 250 chapters and 200,000 members nationwide.

◆ *Alpha Kappa Psi (www.akpsi.com).* Dedicated to promoting and maintaining high standards of education, integrity, and leadership, Alpha Kappa Psi is recognized, in its own words, "as the premier developer of principled business leaders."

◆ *Pi Sigma Epsilon (www.pse.org).* This fraternity serves business students whose focus is sales and marketing. More than 2,000 collegiate members participate in 50 Pi Sigma Epsilon chapters nationwide, with each chapter operating as a small business advised by faculty, local alumni, and other professionals.

In addition to these collegiate organizations, countless professional organizations dedicated to serving business professionals exist. Here are just a few:

◆ American Bankers Association (www.aba.com)

◆ American Finance Association (www.afajof.org)

◆ American Institute of Certified Public Accountants (www.aicpa.org)

◆ American Management Association (www.amanet.org)

◆ Association for Financial Professionals (www.afponline.org)

◆ Association of Fundraising Professionals (www.afpnet.org)

◆ Association of Independent Consultants (www.aiconsult.ca)

◆ Association of International Professionals (www.training professionals.com)

◆ Business and Professional Women USA (www.bpwusa.org)

◆ Commercial Finance Association (www.cfa.com)

◆ Council of Insurance Agents and Brokers (www.ciab.com)

◆ emarketing Association (www.emarketingassociation.com)

◆ Financial Management Association (www.fma.org)

◆ Institute of Management Consultants (www.imcusa.org)

◆ National Association of Securities Dealers, Inc. (www.nasd.com)

- National Mail Order Association (www.nmoa.org)
- Office and Professional Employees International Union (www. opeiu.org)
- Public Relations Society of America (www.prsa.org)
- Recruiter's Network (www.recruitersnetwork.com)
- Securities Industry Association (www.sia.com)
- Society for Human Resource Management (www.shrm.org)
- Society for Nonprofit Organizations (http://danenet.wicip.org/snpo)

If none of these associations apply to you, don't give up hope. A great way to locate a match is to visit one of the following two sites, which feature loads of association listings:

- *Associations on the Net (www.ipl.org/div/aon).* The Internet Public Library has compiled this directory of organizations with a Web presence. Simply click a category to drill down to your field of interest.

- *The ASAE Gateway to Associations Directory (www.asaenet.org/ cda/asae/associations_search/1,3200,MEN3,00.html?AlliedSociety Code=ALL&submit=Go%21).* Search for an association by name, interest area, geographic location, or some combination thereof.

Periodicals for Business Majors

If you're interested in keeping abreast of business news as you engage in your studies, consider any one of the following print publications or their online counterparts (where applicable):

- *Barrons* (www.barrons.com)
- *Business 2.0* (www.business2.com)
- *Business Week* (www.businessweek.com)
- *The Economist* (www.economist.com)
- *Entrepreneur* (www.entrepreneur.com)

◆ *Fast Company* (www.fastcompany.com)

◆ *The Financial Times* (www.ft.com)

◆ *Forbes* (www.forbes.com)

◆ *Fortune* (www.fortune.com)

◆ *Inc.* (www.inc.com)

◆ *Kiplinger's* (www.kiplinger.com)

◆ *Money* (http://money.cnn.com)

◆ *The Wall Street Journal* (www.wsj.com)

In addition, there are, of course, countless business-related publications geared toward serving a particular geographic location or industry. Unfortunately, space does not permit a comprehensive listing of these types of publications in this book.

Handy Websites for the Job Hunter

The World Wide Web has opened a vast sea of information to anyone who has access to a computer. This section cites several Web resources designed to help students find jobs and hammer out a résumé and cover letter. (Of course, these sites aren't the only ones that the business major will find handy; see the other sections in this appendix for additional relevant Web addresses.)

JOB SEARCH/INDUSTRY INFORMATION

◆ AdJobsInc.com (www.adjobsinc.com)

◆ AfterCollege (www.aftercollege.com)

◆ AlumniRecruiter.com (www.alumnirecruiter.com)

◆ BankingBoard.com (www.bankingboard.com)

◆ BankJobs.com (www.bankjobs.com)

◆ CampusCareerCenter.com (www.campuscareercenter.com)

- CareerBank.com (www.careerbank.com)
- CareerBuilder (www.careerbuilder.com)
- CollegeGrad.com (www.collegegrad.com)
- DirectEmployers.com (http://directemployers.com)
- eFinancialCareers (www.efinancialcareers.com)
- Financial Jobs (www.financial-jobs.com)
- First Steps in the Hunt (www.interbiznet.com/hunt/companies)
- GreatInsuranceJobs.com (www.greatinsurancejobs.com)
- IFSjobs.com (www.ifsjobs.com)
- Insurance Job Channel (www.insurancejobchannel.com)
- InternJobs.com (www.internjobs.com)
- InternWeb (www.internweb.com)
- Jobs in the Money (www.jobsinthemoney.com)
- MarketingJobs.com (www.marketingjobs.com)
- Monster.com (www.monster.com)
- MonsterTRAK (www.monstertrak.monster.com)
- Princeton Review's Online Internship Database (www.princeton review.com/cte/search/careerSearch.asp)
- Quint Careers (www.quintcareers.com)
- The Quintessential Directory of Company Career Centers (www. quintcareers.com/career_centers)
- Salary.com (www.salary.com)
- SalesJobs.com (www.salesjobs.com)
- StreetJobs.com (www.streetjobs.com)
- Talent Zoo (www.talentzoo.com)
- Vault (www.vault.com)

◆ WetFeet (www.wetfeet.com)

◆ Yahoo! HotJobs (www.hotjobs.com)

RÉSUMÉ AND COVER LETTER RESOURCES

◆ Bucknell University Cover Letter Checklist (www.departments. bucknell.edu/career_dev/job_search/cover_checklist.shtml)

◆ Career Lab Cover Letter Library (www.careerlab.com/letters/ default.htm)

◆ CollegeGrad.com's Best College Cover Letters (www.collegegrad. com/book/4-0.shtml)

◆ Monster.com Résumé Center (http://resume.monster.com)

◆ Susan Ireland Résumés (http://susanireland.com)

◆ Vault.com Résumé Review, Career Coaching, and Outplacement (www.vault.com/careerservices/careerservices.jsp)

Books for Further Reading

For further reading, business majors should check out the following books on a range of business-related subjects, including general business, landing a job, and interviewing/writing résumés and cover letters.

GENERAL BUSINESS

◆ Barron-Tieger, Barbara and Tieger, Paul D. *Do What You Are: Discover the Perfect Career for You Through the Secrets of Personality Type.* Little, Brown, 2001.

◆ Bolles, Richard Nelson. *What Color Is Your Parachute? 2004: A Practical Manual for Job-Hunters & Career-Changers.* Ten Speed Press, 2003.

◆ Buckingham, Marcus and Coffman, Curt. *First, Break All the Rules: What the World's Greatest Managers Do Differently.* Simon & Schuster, 1999.

◆ Butler, Timothy and Waldroop, James. *Discovering Your Career in Business*. Perseus Books Group, 1997.

◆ Carnegie, Dale. *How to Win Friends and Influence People*. Pocket, 1990.

◆ Collins, Jim. *Good to Great: Why Some Companies Make the Leap . . . and Others Don't*. HarperBusiness, 2001.

◆ Covey, Stephen R. *The 7 Habits of Highly Effective People*. Free Press, 1990.

◆ Friedman, Thomas L. *The Lexus and the Olive Tree: Understanding Globalization*. Anchor, 2000.

◆ Gale, Linda. *Discover What You're Best At*. Fireside, 1998.

◆ Jansen, Julie. *I Don't Know What I Want, but I Know It's Not This: A Step-By-Step Guide to Finding Gratifying Work*. Penguin Books, 2003.

◆ Levinson, Jay Conrad. *Guerilla Marketing: Secrets for Making Big Profits from Your Small Business, 3rd Edition*. Houghton Mifflin, 1998.

◆ Lewis, Michael. *Liar's Poker: Rising Through the Wreckage on Wall Street*. Penguin Books, 1990.

◆ Lore, Nicholas. *The Pathfinder: How to Choose or Change Your Career for a Lifetime of Satisfaction and Success*. Fireside, 1998.

◆ Rolfe, John and Troob, Peter. *Monkey Business: Swinging Through the Wall Street Jungle*. Warner Business Books, 2001.

◆ Yate, Martin. *CareerSmarts: Jobs with a Future*. Balantine Books, 1997.

LANDING A JOB

◆ Aspatore, Jonathan R. *Vault Guide to Starting Your Own Business, 3rd Edition*. Vault.com, 2002.

◆ Field, Shelly. *100 Best Careers for the 21st Century, 2nd Edition*. Arco, 1999.

◆ Hamadeh, Samer; Lerner, Marcy; and Oldman, Mark. *Vault Guide to Top Internships*. Vault, Inc., 2004.

◆ Hardy, Doug and Taylor, Jeff. *Monster Careers: How to Land the Job of Your Life*. Penguin USA, 2004.

◆ Krueger, Brian D. *College Grad Job Hunter: Insider Techniques and Tactics for Finding a Top-Paying Entry Level Job, 5th Edition*. Adams Media Corporation, 2003.

◆ Lerner, Marcy and Shen, Ed. *Vault Guide to Schmoozing, 3rd Edition*. Vault.com, 2002.

◆ Lucht, John. *Rites of Passage at $100,000 to $1 Million+: Your Insider's Lifetime Guide to Executive Job-Changing and Faster Career Progress in the 21st Century*. Viceroy Press, 2000.

◆ Naficy, Mariam. *Fast Track: The Insider's Guide to Winning Jobs in Management Consulting, Investment Banking, and Securities Trading*. Broadway Books, 1997.

◆ Yate, Martin. *Knock 'em Dead 2005: The Ultimate Job Seekers Guide*. Adams Media Corporation, 2004.

INTERVIEWING/RÉSUMÉS AND COVER LETTERS

◆ Asher, Donald. *From College to Career: Entry-Level Resumes for Any Major From Accounting to Zoology, 2nd Edition*. Wetfeet.com, 1999.

◆ DeLuca, Matthew J. *Best Answers to the 201 Most Frequently Asked Interview Questions*. McGraw-Hill, 1996.

◆ Hansen, Katharine. *Dynamic Cover Letters for New Graduates*. Ten Speed Press, 1998.

◆ Hansen, Katharine and Hansen, Randall. *Dynamic Cover Letters Revised, 2nd Edition*. Ten Speed Press, 2001.

◆ Ireland, Susan. *The Complete Idiot's Guide to the Perfect Resume, 3rd Edition*. Alpha Books, 2003.

◆ Ireland, Susan. *The Complete Idiot's Guide to the Perfect Cover Letter*. Alpha Books, 1997.

◆ Kador, John. *201 Best Questions to Ask on Your Interview.* McGraw-Hill, 2002.

◆ Kennedy, Joyce Lain. *Cover Letters For Dummies, 2nd Edition.* John Wiley & Sons, 2000.

◆ Leifman, Howard and Lerner, Marcy. *Vault Guide to Resumes, Cover Letters & Interviewing, 3rd Edition.* Vault.com, 2003.

Additional Help for Choosing a Career

Not sure which career is right for you? Consider taking a career aptitude test, either at your college's career center or online. Here are a few sites of interest:

◆ *AnalyzeMyCareer.com (www.analyzemycareer.com).* Take a career aptitude test, a personality test, and an occupational interest test here. Assessments cost $19.95 each, or all three for $49.95.

◆ *Assessment.com (www.assessment.com).* This site offers a career aptitude test. Simply register, answer 71 questions, and then view your report online free of charge. (For a fee, you can view even more detailed information about your career aptitude.)

◆ *College911.com (www.college911.com/express/precog3/index.asp).* Find your life's purpose by answering the questions on this page. The test is free.

Index

NOTES